For the Muslims

For the Muslims

Islamophobia in France

by
Edwy Plenel

Translated by
David Fernbach

VERSO
London • New York

First published in English by Verso 2016
Translation © David Fernbach 2016
First published as *Pour les musulmans*
© Editions La Découverte 2014, 2016

1 3 5 7 9 10 8 6 4 2

Verso
UK: 6 Meard Street, London W1F 0EG
US: 20 Jay Street, Suite 1010, Brooklyn, NY 11201
versobooks.com

Verso is the imprint of New Left Books

ISBN-13: 978-1-78478-486-7
ISBN-13: 978-1-78478-488-1 (US EBK)
ISBN-13: 978-1-78478-487-4 (UK EBK)

British Library Cataloguing in Publication Data
A catalogue record for this book is available from the British Library

Library of Congress Cataloging-in-Publication Data

Names: Plenel, Edwy, author. | Fernbach, David, translator.
Title: For the Muslims : Islamophobia in France / by Edwy Plenel ; translated
  by David Fernbach.
Other titles: Pour les musulmans. English
Description: Brooklyn, NY : Verso, 2016.
Identifiers: LCCN 2016005821 | ISBN 9781784784867 (pbk. : alk. paper)
Subjects: LCSH: Muslims – France – Social conditions. | Muslims – France – Ethnic
  identity. | Islam and politics – France. | National characteristics, French.
Classification: LCC DC34.5.M87 P5413 2016 | DDC 305.6/970944 – dc23
LC record available at http://lccn.loc.gov/2016005821

Typeset in Fournier by MJ&N Gavan, Truro, Cornwall
Printed and bound by CPI Group (UK) Ltd, Croydon, CR0 4YY

To Edgar Morin, who has shown the Way

Each man carries the entire form of the human condition.
— Montaigne, *Essays*, Book 3,
Chapter 2, 'Of repenting'

The Republic is invaded by reactionaries of every kind, they worship it with a brutal and terrible love, they embrace it in order to stifle it.

— Émile Zola, *Lettre à la France*, 7 January 1898

CONTENTS

Preface: Against Hatred

The first edition of *Pour les musulmans* was published in September 2014. With official ceremonies and presidential speeches, France was then remembering the fatal chain of events that had dragged Europe and the whole world along with it into catastrophe, blindness and massacre a century before. These commemorations, recalling the warnings that, far from being heeded at the time, were scoffed at and slandered, should have served as an alarm against bellicose slogans of national identity. Slogans that lead peoples to abdicate clarity of mind to the point of abandoning their own humanity.

We need only listen again to Jean Jaurès, whose murder on 31 July 1914 heralded the eclipse of European reason. To remember, for example, the 'Speech to the youth' that the founder of French socialism delivered at the Lycée Albi in 1903. 'Courage', Jaurès said, 'does not mean maintaining over the world the terrible cloud of war, which, while still dormant, one can always flatter oneself will explode on others. Courage does not mean leaving in the hands of force the solution to the conflicts that reason can resolve.

Courage means the exaltation of man, not his abdication.' Jaurès emphasized that courage meant 'seeking and telling the truth; not accepting the law of the triumphant lie, and not echoing, with our soul, our mouth and our hands, the imbecile applause and fanatical cries'. This is what he called 'breaking the circle of fatality, the iron circle, the circle of hatred, in which even just demands provoke reprisals that boast of being similarly just, in which war follows war in a movement without end or solution, in which law and violence, clad in the same bloody livery, can hardly be told apart, and in which a torn humanity weeps at the victory of justice almost as much as at its defeat.'

A year has passed since this centenary of the start of Europe's brutalization at its own hand, with its nationalist passions and deadly identities bent on diverting peoples from common democratic and social causes by creating scapegoats for their resentments. And it is clear enough that in France this pedagogy of memory was not enough to prevent the start of a repetition of the same tragic errors in the face of the world's uncertainties, its unpredictable pitfalls and unexpected dangers. As if our leaders today, despite being the official heirs of that French socialism inaugurated by Jaurès, fiercely reject his legacy. They have neither learned nor understood anything from him.

From the attacks in Paris of January 2015 to the massacres of November 2015, this book has been overtaken by the threat that it sought to forestall: the bloody feasts of hatred and fear in which crimes of terrorism pave the way for the state of exception. As a plea against the growing stigmatizing of my compatriots of Islamic culture or belief, collectively identified with a violence for which they are fundamentally not to blame, *Pour les musulmans* was not enough to trigger the awareness that it called for. Not only have Islamophobic actions increased in the wake of the Paris attacks, but prejudice towards Muslims, essentialized en bloc despite their profound diversity, has grown increasingly banal within the ambit of a public debate polarized by the far right, espousing its agenda and subject to its hegemony even in the electoral arena.

The book's detractors scarcely took the trouble to read it, condemning it simply for its title. As if standing up for France's Muslims was not a gesture of fraternity with people who are just like us, but an act of collaboration with the enemy. Prejudice makes people lazy. Unable to accept a rational and informed debate, they avoid it by invective, slander and anathema. At best, I was classed among the useful idiots of an undefined 'Islamism', deprived of history and complexity and reduced to terror alone. At worst, stereotyped and essentialized in my turn, I was identified with the 'anti-France' dear to our far right, this spectre brandished for the purpose of an appeal to national purification by the eradication of all difference and the elimination of all dissidence.

For these sowers of discord, harbingers of a civil war of which the people in all their diversity would be the first victims, the builders of bridges and weavers of ties are priority targets. The first voices they want to silence, by caricaturing and disqualifying them, are those that call for dialogue and encounter, knowledge and discovery. Those that, arguing against a competition in victimhood, spread the lesson of commonality and shared injustices, without distinction of origin or belief, belonging or appearance.

It was from this point of view that *Pour les musulmans* was found to be so disturbing. All the more so as, by echoing Zola's 'Pour les Juifs', it refused to set one suffering against another, Islamophobia against anti-Semitism, calling on the contrary for the victims of racist and xenophobic passions to understand how their destinies are linked, how intolerance is like a nest of Russian dolls, its targets being all minorities, all difference, all dissidence. In different latitudes and with many faces, from Marine Le Pen to Donald Trump, not to mention Vladimir Putin, Islamophobia today fulfills the cultural function that fell yesterday to anti-Semitism, in the last crisis of Western modernity: to impose the ideological hegemony of a national identity of exclusion and rejection, intolerant towards minorities. By setting up, and feeding prejudice against, the figure of the 'enemy within' – unassimilable, foreign, corrupting, threatening, etc. – the national body can be forced into a single identity, defined and defended from above, which blocks any challenge to the established order.

'Worse than the noise of boots, the silence of slippers': this remark, attributed to the Swiss writer Max Frisch, could sum up the message of *For the Muslims*. It is a warning cry against indifference: the eyes that turn away, the voices that fall silent, the hands that avoid contact – in other words, the lack of fraternity. But it is also a challenge to politicians of both left and right, whose blindness, far from guiding us away from catastrophe, is leading us towards it: the compromises with an ever more extreme right and the abdication of a rightward-veering left, each of these abandoning the true dynamic of the French republican promise, its democratic exigency and social ambition. For more than thirty years since the electoral breakthrough of the National Front in 1984, this drift, far from blocking the threat of the far right with its xenophobia and racism, has made this acceptable, by sharing its obsessions and validating its themes. Placing themselves squarely on the terrain of their supposed adversary, these politicians focused on short-term survival have steadily legitimized it, adopting even its single-minded stigmatization of those compatriots who, by their belief, culture or origin, have in common the toxic word: Islam.

For the Muslims is thus an appeal to forestall the approaching disaster, in hopes that all those of good democratic will can unite to avoid a *politique du pire*. Sadly, we are still far from this, to judge by the grim balance-sheet of 2015, marked by the tragic competition between a totalitarian terrorism and the politics of fear that it conjures up and provokes. This forward flight, in which the executive power strengthens its grip on society, dismissing and muzzling its concerns, has culminated in a general retreat of fundamental liberties, in the form of an indefinite state of emergency whose targets are indistinct: environmental activists as much as suspected Islamists. To this must be added a rise in unemployment, precariousness and poverty that arouses no official emotion, as if the terrorist event allowed the social emergency to be eclipsed. Not forgetting, as a final offering to the far right, the sudden promotion on the left under François Hollande of the same poison of national identity as was brandished on the right under Nicolas Sarkozy: the stripping of French nationality as a weapon of national purification.

Failure to learn from history means making the future fragile. Those responses which, out of ideological or tactical calculation, profit from fear for purposes of domestic politics, may be inviting disaster in due course. Violating the very democracy they claim to defend against adversaries who hate it, speaking the same language of annihilation, eradication and destruction as the latter, accustoming our own society to lower its guard on fundamental liberties – all this is not a show of our strength, but rather a proof of our weakness. It is to fall into the trap of the terrorists, like rabbits blinded by the headlights. It is to espouse their temporality, which is one of a monstrous and paralysing present, a present with neither past nor future. A dead present.

By insisting right away that 'France is at war,' as an axiom that needs no demonstration, the president of the French republic and the head of the armed forces made precisely this choice on 16 November 2015, before the parliamentarians met in congress at Versailles. Devoted exclusively to security issues, his speech was doubly blind: blind to causes, and thus to the past; blind to solutions, and thus to the future. The only perspective he proposed was the immediate one of war, not just in the distance but close at hand, right here. Being without memory, this is a dead end. Ignoring the contexts, genealogies and legacies that shaped the threat, this response is short-sighted and will soon fail. Beneath the determined appearance, it proceeds as though in a vacuum: not only disconnected from the international origins of the drama but also, what is more serious, oblivious to the national consequences of its stubbornness.

It runs a strong risk, therefore, of achieving nothing but the perpetuation, not to say extension, of the catastrophe, as already predicted by all specialists, researchers or diplomats, experts in geopolitics or intelligence veterans, whose conclusion is unanimous: France is suffering today a boomerang effect. The unprecedented event that fills us all with terror, this violence unleashed against an open and diverse society, is the fruit of decades of strategic mistakes, from the wars in Afghanistan and Iraq to the compromises with dictatorial regimes and obscurantist monarchies, not forgetting the mishandling of the Palestinian cause.

By embarking on the same tragically false route, symbolized by the American adventure in Iraq in 2003, our rulers have dangerously exposed a French democracy that is already fragile enough. Weakened by a confiscatory presidential regime, the legacy of French Bonapartism, it is poorly equipped to resist authoritarian temptation. Moreover, it has been poisoned for too long by the dissemination of an anti-republican imaginary in which identity supplants equality, security overrides liberty, and the fear of others destroys human fraternity. If the American blunder damaged the whole world, by virtue of the power of the United States, the French error risks above all ruining our own country, wounding its democracy, and even lending a helping hand to its gravediggers.

'Just be afraid, and we'll take care of everything' is what we are now told by a police state that imposes itself on the rule of law, making distrust towards a pluralistic, vigilant and mobilized society into a lasting principle of survival. The terrorists could not have dreamed of a more symbolic victory: the invitation to desert democracy and blindly delegate our power, the better to lose it for good. It is this chain of events that we have to refuse, since, rather than protecting us, it leaves us vulnerable and exposed. This position of principle, far from being irresponsible, safeguards the future.

Safeguarding the future was the concern of one Frenchman who, during the First World War, continued to voice, despite the clash of weapons, the warning launched by Jean Jaurès. 'You think of victory,' he wrote. 'I think of the peace that will follow ... Do not break all the bridges, as we shall still have to cross the river. Do not destroy the future. Even a deep wound, if clean, will heal; but don't poison it. Let us take a stand against hatred.'

This was Romain Rolland, awarded the Nobel Prize for literature in 1915. In November of that year he published the book that earned him so much anathema and abuse: *Above the Battle*. Rolland rejected with all his soul the unanimous support for the war that led intellectuals, both French and German, to deny their common humanity, each arrogating to their own side the privileged status of a civilization pitted against barbarism, on which the enemy camp had a natural monopoly. Refusing to 'include in the same reprobation the German people and their military or intellectual leaders', Rolland was then one of the rare spirits to take a stand against hatred.

Until his final proof corrections, Rolland was going to call this text *Against Hatred*. When peace came in 1918, with its portion of injustice and humiliation, the first stir-rings of a universal conscience coalesced around its author, whose solitary dissidence amid the hell of war had shone like a light showing a path to the future. That conscience was articulated in the 'Declaration of the Independence of Mind', published in *L'Humanité* on 26 June 1919, whose signatories included Bertrand Russell along with Stefan Zweig, Albert Einstein, Heinrich Mann, Benedetto Croce, Léon Werth, Upton Sinclair, Rabindranath Tagore and many others. Their appeal to a 'fraternal union' of intellec-tuals from all cultures and nations against 'the almost total abdication of the world's intelligence and its subjugation to unleashed forces' ended with a paean to 'the free mind, one and multiple, eternal'.

In the opening pages of *Above the Battle*, Romain Rolland confided that 'I have found myself, for the last year, very rich in enemies. I have this to say to them: they may hate me, but they will not teach me to hate.' And he went on to urge his readers to 'stand up against a hatred which is deadlier still than war, for it is an infection produced by its wounds, and does as much harm to the person possessing it as to the one it pursues'.

A century later, in another epoch and faced with dif-ferent wars, it is the same demand that we need, and that the present book seeks to put forward: not to surrender to hatred.

Paris, December 2015

1

'There is a problem with Islam in France,' I heard one morning in June 2014 on the main French public radio station. This was not a marginal statement but that of a major contemporary commentator, invited by the editors to spout without contradiction the obsession that takes the place of thought with him. This 'problem with Islam' is nothing less than a 'concern for civilization', he added, regretting that such concern has been 'abandoned to the National Front'. With the moral authority that his status as an esteemed guest speaker conferred, he thus invited the government parties of both right and left to recklessly take up the agenda of the far right.

As we know, the devil is in the detail, in this case the vagaries of the calendar. It happened to be the Monday after Whitsun, the Christian festival that commemorates the descent of the Holy Spirit onto the apostles of Jesus of Nazareth, thus annexing Shavuot, one of the three pilgrimage feasts of Judaism, which itself arose from the age-old harvest cycle. In Christian tradition, the Holy Spirit takes the form of tongues of fire that descend from the sky in a tumultuous wind and by alighting on each of the apostles transform them into polyglots, able to speak all the languages on earth. Despite our awareness of the dominating and oppressive universalism that would follow, how can we not hear in this scene of early Christianity the echo of a world of diversity, respect and concern for others?

There was nothing of this that morning, when I heard just one language closed to all others, a language of rejection and exclusion, of astounding violence beneath its apparent restraint. It was the decorous language of discrimination: a language of ignorance, that on the grounds of their religion views with the same wholesale disapproval men, women and children, no matter their diversity and plurality; a language of prejudice, that manufactures the foreigner as foreign by essentializing groups of human beings on the basis of their origin, culture, faith, belonging and birth.

Celebrity can be disastrous even more often than old age. There are honours that conceal defeat, distinctions that tell of renunciation. The words I heard, both baneful and detestable, were those of a member of the Académie Française, Alain Finkielkraut, just recently promoted to this 'immortal' status. The self-proclaimed spokesperson of the 'French born and bred' [*Français de souche*], against the threat of a 'great replacement'[1] theorized by his accomplice

---

1   'The great replacement' [*le grand remplacement*] is a far-right conspiracy theory, rooted in neo-Nazi theories of the 1950s, regarding an alleged policy promoted by the French state, élites and the like to systematically replace the white French population with North and Sub-Saharan African populations, through mass immigration and demographic growth. The theory has been popularized by Renaud Camus (formerly a member

in xenophobic regression, Renaud Camus, Finkielkraut is not only the standard-bearer of a conservative thought that vituperates against modernity in all its forms. He has also become a respectable authority for the most common-place racist clichés, accompanied by a blind reduction of anti-racist vigilance to anti-Semitism alone, renunciation of which is apparently enough to transform the far right into a respectable political party.

Yet he has in the past been less careful, particularly at the time of the urban riots in 2005, whose social causes were widely documented by journalists and researchers, along with the police actions that sparked them off. In an off-the-cuff interview with the Israeli daily *Haaretz*, confirmed by the newspaper despite Finkielkraut's subsequent attempt at retraction, the future academician expressed his alarm at seeing the 'barbarians' at our gates, and denounced 'a revolt of an ethno-religious character'. 'The generous idea of a war on racism', he concluded, 'has gradually undergone a monstrous transformation into a lying ideology. Anti-racism will be to the twenty-first century what communism was in the twentieth.' By which he means, a criminal ideology.

No accident then if, faced with the outrage that this declaration provoked, Nicolas Sarkozy, still only interior minister, but whose incendiary attitude was not without its effect on the spread of the rioting, hastened to come to the aid of this 'intellectual who is a credit to French

of the Socialist Party), who has come under fire for the anti-Semitism expressed in his texts, such as his diaries published by Éditions Fayard [*translator*].

intelligence'. Sarkozy added his own descant against the 'dictatorship of fine feelings', an evocative formula which actually sounds like an invitation to support a regime of bad feelings, proud of its hatreds and exclusions, mocking kindness and disqualifying generosity. 'An indispensable intellectual', chorused the *académiciens* who elected the author of *L'Identité malheureuse* to join their number in 2014. 'One of our most brilliant intellectuals', Sarkozy added in approving their decision – Sarkozy who despite the various legal cases against him will be remembered as the inventor of a ministry of 'national identity'.

Origin gives no protection from anything. Only lives, their paths and coherence, stand as evidence. We once knew a different Finkielkraut. A long time ago, in 1980, he launched in *Le Juif imaginaire* a 'plea for the indeterminable', urging people to 'think the world in its totality' rather than reduce it to pre-assigned identities, predetermined places, immutable origins, nations closed in on themselves. Very likely this is the common individual tragedy of an unsatisfied quest for recognition, which sometimes haunts a persecuted minority and even its heirs: the fatigue produced by the uncomfortable position of pariah, giving way to the zeal of the parvenu. A parvenu who can never do enough in his yearning to be at last distinguished and accepted, at the risk of losing himself. Losing his history, his memory, his inheritance.

2

'There is a problem with Islam in France ...' It was hearing for the nth time this refrain which, unchallenged, sets France at war against a religion, acclimatizing it to prejudice, accustoming it to indifference – in short, habituating it to the worst, that decided me to write this book. Faced with the growing acceptability of a discourse similar to that which, before the European catastrophe, maintained the existence of a 'Jewish problem' in France, I wanted to respond by resolutely taking the side of our compatriots of Muslim origin, culture or faith, against those who make them into scapegoats for our disquiets and uncertainties.

My particular concern is with those in high places, as xenophobic passions are never generated spontaneously, but always aroused and maintained by more basic defeats, defeats of thinking. People who, given their own social comfort, have no excuse for their blindness such as their condition or their environment, their misery or their distress, however unpardonable this ultimately may be. People who should enlighten, educate and elevate, and not stupefy, excite or enervate. People who claim to know, who assure

us that they reflect upon matters, who want to rule; yet
whom the present time, with its challenges and uncertainties, has rendered ignorant, stupid and dangerous. For want
of knowledge, thought and ability, they have nothing else
to propose than a mortifying passion concealed beneath
obsessive Islamophobia: the sorry passion for inequality,
hierarchy and discrimination. A destructive passion which,
at the end of the day, will not spare anyone in its ineluctable
ble mission to sort, separate and select among our common
humanity. A regressive and destructive passion that under-
mines and ruins the hope of emancipation, whose motor
has always been the equality of rights.

It took the European catastrophe of two world wars and
their crimes against humanity for the French Constitution
– initially that of the Fourth Republic, maintained by its
successor – to inscribe in the first article of its preamble:
'In the wake of the victory achieved by free peoples over
regimes that sought to enslave and degrade the human
person, the French people proclaim once more that every
human being, without distinction of race, religion or belief,
possesses inalienable and sacred rights.' It is this promise,
this wisdom painfully acquired, that is today endangered
by the habituation to hatred, discrimination, exclusion,
rejection, violence, etc., that has established itself in France
with the ever greater acceptance of anti-Muslim discourses
and actions.

In 2013, the National Consultative Commission on
Human Rights (CNCDH) referred in its annual report
on racism, anti-Semitism and xenophobia to an 'upsurge
of violence'. And, in this upsurge, the rise of anti-Muslim

intolerance and polarization against Islam was the most constant and well-established aspect. 'If our epoch is compared with the pre-war period, it could be said that today the Muslim, closely followed by the North African, has replaced the Jew in the representations and construction of a scapegoat,' commented the sociologists and political scientists whose views were solicited by the Commission.

A year later, in 2014, the same CNCDH raised the level of its warning, observing the resurgence in France of a 'brutal, biology-inflected racism that scapegoats the foreigner', accompanied by a sharp rise in anti-Muslim incidents. It is no coincidence that the steady fall in the global index of tolerance measured by this Commission, of twelve points in the course of four years, began in 2009, the year of the supposed debate on national identity, a consecration of two years of Sarkozy's miseducation. Racism and xenophobia are not generated spontaneously; they are the product of a policy that yields to them. 'The way in which we speak about immigrants and minorities, along with alacrity in defending them and coming down hard on xenophobic statements, are essential in preventing individuals from (re)lapsing into prejudice,' stressed this annual report for 2014, expressing alarm above all at the trivialization of Islamophobia under cover of a supposed struggle for 'secularism'. The CNCDH went on to observe:

Racism has undergone a profound change of paradigm in the postcolonial period, with a slippage from biological racism to cultural racism. Hiding in this new guise, the term 'Islamophobia' has been used by political

groups to mobilize a wider electorate and demand the
right to express its hatred of Muslims and the Islamic
religion. Still more disturbing, a certain radical fringe
is taking the step from speech to action. According to
them, Islamophobia is a matter of freedom of opinion
and expression, and on these grounds the expressions of
hatred it may inspire, whether towards the Islamic religion or its believers, do not fall under the scope of the
criminal code. Following this dangerous line of argument, aggression against a veiled woman is simply a
political act against a practice seen as a form of oppression of women.

Setting itself against this vicious tendency, the CNCDH
sought therefore to 'name what we denounce and wish to
combat'. Islamophobia, in other words the phenomenon
that targets Islam and Muslims and is expressed 'by way of
negative opinions and prejudices, often giving rise to rejection, exclusion and discrimination, insulting or defamatory
expressions, incitement to hatred, damage to property with
a symbolic value, and sometimes even aggression'.

It is necessary therefore to raise one's voice, since these
institutional warnings failed to prevent the propagation of
anti-Muslim prejudice on the airwaves of Radio France or
from the armchairs of the Académie Française. To raise
one's voice, in defence not only of Muslims but of all other
minorities that this habituation to hatred of the Other
places in danger, exposes and renders vulnerable. The
anti-Semitic crimes, aggression against black people and
anti-Roma violence that in recent years have attested to a

deadly intolerance cannot be disassociated from a growing tolerance of everyday speech and mundane acts of discrimination and exclusion towards French Muslims.

Racism is like a monstrous set of Russian dolls, a Pandora's Box that, once opened, spares no target. And it is by the routine targeting of Muslims, in the guise of a rejection of their religion, that it has once more found a home and become acceptable. Tolerable, respectable and socially within the pale. The extension of the domain of hatred that we are stunned witnesses of today springs from this decorous spread of anti-Muslim racism to occupy the place left vacant by the unacceptability of anti-Semitism – an appreciable victory despite being so belatedly won.

Since the end of the last decade, argues the researcher and historian Valérie Igounet, author of *Histoire du négationnisme en France*, a standard work on the far right, 'the enemy of the National Front is no longer the Jew but the French Muslim.' 'The Islamophobic marker', she went on to explain in an interview with *Mediapart*, 'has replaced that of anti-Semitism. The message is recontextualized and can be conveyed in a few words: the Islamist danger is opposed to the secular values that are championed by our country and are the foundation of the French Republic. It is also a way of getting round anti-racist legislation: to speak of Islam is a way of speaking of immigration without risking legal sanction.'

The trap is a crude one, but sadly it works. The far right has in no way modified its stock-in-trade which consists in fuelling fears and hatreds, in designating scapegoats. But it has changed its target, with the intuition that, in the

confusion of the time and the disturbance of minds, a xenophobic movement can obtain respectability if it takes its
distance from anti-Semitism. That was 'the thing to get rid
of', as Louis Aliot, vice-president of the National Front,
explained to Igounet. Pulling no punches, he explained
that 'de-demonizing only concerns anti-Semitism.' 'When
passing out leaflets in the street, I saw that neither immigration nor Islam was a glass ceiling. Other people are worse
than we are on those topics. It is only anti-Semitism that
prevents people from voting for us. The moment you get
rid of that ideological catch, you free up the rest.'

The 'rest', then, all the rest that we allow to be said and
done, abandoning its targets to silence, indifference and
invisibility. Time is short, and we cannot say that we had
not been forewarned. Our country has today become a
European exception, with a far right ensconced at the centre
of public debate to the point of preparing itself for the conquest of power, an 'official' right in moral decomposition,
beset by ideological disarray and financial corruption, and
a left crushed to pulp, more of a minority than ever, more
divided than ever, and in still greater disarray. Elsewhere in
Europe, particularly in Greece, Spain and Italy, the financial, economic, social, ecological, European, etc., crisis has
unleashed a variety of new alternatives, giving strength
to the confrontation between rediscovered progress
and stoked-up fear that is both necessary and inevitable.
France, however, has an empty space there, facilitating an
unexpected return of the inegalitarian ideologies which,
protected by identitarian retrenchment, ravaged our continent last century.

For the first time since their defeat in 1945, which compelled the French right to convert to the Republic, now constitutionally proclaimed 'democratic and social', they have now firmly emerged from being a marginal minority and can impose on all the rest of the political field the hegemony of their old rhetoric: identity against equality. The frozen order of the one against the creative movement of the other. An identity of closure and exclusion against an equality of openness and relationship; the exacerbation of the national against the fraternity of the social; the hierarchy of origins, appearance and belonging, belief and culture, against the perspective of rights and possibilities for all, which has constantly to be renewed and won.

Under the pretext of protection from the foreigner, an outside threat that inevitably takes the face of the enemy within (yesterday the Jew, today the Muslim or, as equivalent, the Arab), this ideology of supposedly national preference proposes the poisonous solution of wholesale rejection, including rejection of France as it now exists and lives. In reality, it is simply an alibi to perpetrate and reinforce domination: while the oppressed make war in the name of their origins, the oppressors can quietly get on with their business, i.e., business. Their private business, to the detriment of public spirit; the mad race to accumulate, which as always leads to inequalities that are genuinely intolerable.

If this sombre rise is fed by the crisis of confidence in a shamefaced Europe that has lost popular legitimacy by identifying with economic competition, it is no less an internal, French story, which began just thirty years ago in 1984, when the National Front made its first significant electoral breakthrough. At that time, the European Union did not yet exist while the Soviet Union still did; the European Economic Community had only ten member states (including Greece but neither Spain nor Portugal), and Germany did not even dare to dream of reunification.

Ever since that time, with few interruptions, the advance of a far right faithful to its past owes nothing to fate and everything to the politicians who lent a helping hand in so many ways: the opportunistic failures of the so-called 'government' parties, whether right or left, that acknowledged the far right's 'genuine issues' around security and xenophobia in order to offer their own, 'better' responses, which at the end of the day only serves to legitimize the priorities of the National Front. Champions in the main of a politics of fear and, for the most obtuse among them, a war of civilizations whose perils are compounded by the weight of a colonial past that has never really been closed, these sorcerer's apprentices endanger our common future.

Our own fate, that of every single one of us, depends on the fate meted out to the Muslims of France, inasmuch as this holds the key to our relationship to the world and to others, whether we loosen or exacerbate its tensions, appease them by reason or inflame them by insisting on a supposed Muslim question. The outcome depends, ultimately, on whether we consider (and accept and respect) our Muslim compatriots in all their diversity, or whether we essentialize them en bloc, amassing everything that derives somehow from Islam into an indistinct menace that legitimates their exclusion or effacement. Far from protecting us, this reduction of French Muslims to a religion itself reduced to terrorism and fundamentalism is a gift to religious radicalization, in a game of mirrors in which xenophobic essentialization justifies identitarian essentialization.

This is the warning I want people to heed, on behalf of Muslims and of the human diversity that this word covers. In defence of all those women and men whom even here in France the prevailing wisdom assimilates to a religion, itself identified with an obscurantist fundamentalism – just as yesterday other human beings were essentialized, caricatured and slandered – in an ideological mélange of ignorance and distrust that paves the way to persecution.

The stake here is not simply solidarity, but fidelity. To our history, to our memory, to our heritage. In defence of the Muslims, therefore, as our predecessors wrote in defence of the Jews, the blacks or the Roma, but also in defence of minorities and the oppressed. In defence, quite simply, of France.

3

To confuse a whole community – of origin, culture or belief – with the acts of a few individuals who appeal to that community or make use of it, is to open the door to injustice. And to allow such discourse to establish itself by way of our silence means accustoming our consciences to exclusion, by accepting the legitimacy of discrimination and the respectability of the amalgam. In the twentieth century, the European tragedy taught us the fateful consequences of this downward spiral, via the passive acceptance of the construction of a 'Jewish question'. If only because we are responsible for that legacy, we refuse with all our soul the insidious and insistent contemporary construction of a 'Muslim question'.

Have we really forgotten the best of ourselves? I mean the awakening of French conscience in the form of a prophetic alarm whose echoes, despite saving one man and a nation, were sadly unable to prevent the catastrophe of genocide. The defence, in the person of a single individual, Alfred Dreyfus, of a people, the Jewish people, with whom he was identified by the intersection of an origin, a culture and a religion. The rejection not just of the state injustice suffered by one army officer, but of the mundane, everyday anti-Semitism by which a hatred of the other was constructed and established, a hatred unaware of itself, in the blind essentializing of a human group depicted in terms of prejudice and fatal caricature.

That past struggle was largely conducted in the press, just as today the question of Islamophobia is above all the responsibility of the mass media, which is where representations are spread and become acceptable in the form of obvious truths, stigmatizing a population of men, women and children on grounds of their religious, spiritual or community identity. While the journalistic profession has not forgotten Émile Zola's famous *J'accuse ...!*, with which on 13 January 1898 in the newspaper *L'Aurore* the author took up the defence of Captain Dreyfus, imprisoned since 14 April 1895 on Devil's Island, in the penal colony of Cayenne in French Guiana, under a false accusation of espionage, it no longer remembers what led up to this – and what actually marked the real turning point for Zola, who had previously been indifferent to Dreyfus's cause.

This was an article Zola published a year and a half earlier, on 16 May 1896, in *Le Figaro*, a paper seldom suspected of radicalism or bold initiative, to which he had been a celebrated contributor since 1880. With the success of *L'Assommoir* in 1877, the writer had become a respectable and respected personality, a '*chevalier*' (1888) and then '*officier*' (1893) of the Légion d'Honneur, president of the Société des Gens de Lettres, candidate to the Académie

Française; in short, a man threatened by 'all the perils of money and fame', as the historian Henri Guillemin would write.

Zola would go on to renounce this illusory 'cultural capital', preferring the eternity of principles, and turn his back on all his right-thinking contemporaries. And the decisive act in his break was this article of 1896, in which the name of Dreyfus was not mentioned, but whose argument led the first Dreyfusards, in particular the journalist Bernard Lazare, to contact Zola in order to rally him to their cause.

This article was entitled, quite simply, 'Pour les Juifs' (with a capital letter), and one need only replace the word 'Jews' in its first lines by the word 'Muslims' to understand the resonance with our own time: it was a cry of anger against a poisoned atmosphere.

'In recent years', Zola began, 'I have been following with mounting surprise and disgust the campaign that people are trying to stir up in France against the Jews. To me this seems a monstrosity, meaning something outside all good sense, all truth and all justice, something so stupid and blind as to take us back centuries, something that would finally lead to the worst abomination, a religious persecution that would stain every country with blood. And I mean this.'

Zola explicitly addresses himself to his own people, as I am very likely doing here, given the extent to which the Muslim question divides our own readers, sometimes even those close to us. He mentions, indeed, those 'friends of mine' who 'say that they cannot endure them [Jews]'. Just as some people around us today cannot endure the public assertion of Muslim religion or identity. Just as other people today portray Islam as a 'problem' for France, a matter of 'civilization'.

Zola's target, then, was not popular prejudice, but the fashionable Parisian anti-Semitism that he came across in the salons. A prejudice echoing that of Édouard Drumont, author of *La France juive*, an abject book published by Flammarion at the author's own expense in 1886, but that became a bestseller after a launch supported precisely by *Le Figaro*. An anti-Semitism that hardly flinched when the same Drumont, in his paper *La Libre Parole* – established in 1892 to wage a paranoid war on 'cosmopolitan Jewry' and subtitled 'La France aux Français! [France for the French!]' – accompanied his denunciation of the 'traitor' Dreyfus by the headline: 'Down with the Jews!' A mainstream sentiment that allowed Drumont to say, as if it were simply self-evident: 'Anti-Semitism is accepted by all thinking people.'

By challenging this, Émile Zola sought to dismantle such prejudices, chiefly the assumption which, on the basis of the old religious anti-Judaism – 'our eighteen centuries of imbecilic persecution' – had become the matrix of modern anti-Semitism: the accusation of being an aloof, separate people whose characteristic motivation was 'love of money'. Anti-Semitic unreason would subsequently enhance this prejudice with the assimilation of Judaism to Bolshevism, of being Jewish to the communist menace, without country or border. Capital on the one hand, communism on the other; in all cases, the Jews to blame for the ills of the world. Just as today, between money and

terrorism, the wealth of obscurantist regimes and the violence of fundamentalist radicals, the Muslims of France
are the object of a universal accusation, blamed for mis-
deeds and crimes that are remote or foreign to them, simply
because of the offence of their community, origin or belief.

Describing this mechanism of global rejection, in which
individuals are negated and particularities fixed and frozen,
Zola sums up the argument that naturalizes a racism whose
targets can always vary according to epoch, context and
circumstances. 'The Jews', he observes, 'are accused of
being a nation within the nation, of leading the separate
life of a religious caste and thus being, across borders, a
kind of international sect, with no real homeland, capable
one day, should it prevail, of seizing control of the world'.
Here we find our present-day fantasies about the 'enemy
within', represented by a menacing Islam indiscriminately
identified with those of our compatriots who are Muslim
by culture or religion. An Islam of violence and power,
terror and finance, intolerance and conquest, for which all
Muslims are collectively responsible.

'That there is a distressing concentration of wealth in
the hands of some Jews is an undisputed fact,' Zola continues. 'But the same can be said of some Catholics and
Protestants. To exploit popular revolt by harnessing it to a
religious passion, and especially to throw Jews to the dogs
to meet the demands of the dispossessed, on the pretext of
their being men of money, is a hypocritical, mendacious
socialism that should be denounced and refuted.' In short,
the writer refused the first step towards rejection of the
Other that consists in freezing her outside of all history,

all contradiction and all pluralism, in brief, denying her liberty.

But Zola went still further, with the luminous prescience of those who are able to put themselves in another's shoes. He glimpsed the self-fulfilling prophecy that is the perverse wellspring of persecution, fuelling it and justifying it in return: the fact that it encourages among its victims, quite logically and legitimately, their own withdrawal, rejection and revolt, in short their resistance, the insider's angry pride and defiance of stigmatization and exclusion, to confront and overcome these. 'We end up creating a danger,' warned Zola, 'by shouting every morning that it exists. By showing the people a scarecrow, the real monster is created.'

What this scarecrow initially serves is our own blindness, the refusal to assume our responsibilities. 'The Jews, as they exist today, are our work, the work of our eighteen centuries of imbecilic persecution,' Zola insists, just as we can assert today that the situation in which French Muslims are placed cannot be dissociated from the long duration of our colonial domination. 'We have struck them, injured them, showered them with injustice and violence,' the author continues, 'and it is scarcely surprising if they cherish in their hearts, albeit unwittingly, the hope of a distant revenge, the will to resist, to preserve themselves and to overcome.'

Zola's 'For the Jews' ends with a vibrant appeal to 'human unity', an upsurge of humanity against 'social malefactors' whose 'quagmire' contains no more than 'religious passion and unbalanced intelligence'. 'Let us disarm our hatreds,' he writes, 'let us love our fellows in our cities, love beyond our borders, work to mix the races into a single family, happy at last! … And let the madmen and the wicked go back to the barbarism of the forests, those who imagine that they can wreak justice with blows of the knife.'

From this point on, the writer's destiny was cast. The Dreyfus affair would give him no peace, leading in 1898 to an exile of nearly a year in London after his condemnation to prison for *J'accuse* …*!* He died in 1902, suffocating in his sleep in his Paris apartment, the victim in all probability of criminal action. The transfer of his remains in 1908 to the Panthéon, where France honours its great men, could not wipe out the extreme violence that his courageous transgression had attracted, expressed once more that very day by an attempted assassination of Alfred Dreyfus with a shot fired by an anti-Dreyfusard journalist.

'I found it cowardly to keep silent,' Zola wrote simply to his wife on the eve of leaving to campaign against 'a hidden poison that is driving us all to madness'. 'This poison is the enraged hatred of Jews that has been fed to the people every morning for years,' he wrote in another article, this way of waving 'the bogey man of the foreigner' which he felt set the stage, beyond the crime against Dreyfus – the innocent condemned, the army perverted – for silent or active acquiescence to a crime against humanity.

'One day France will thank me for having helped to save its honour,' Zola declared to his judges. From Jews to Muslims, from yesterday to today, it is easy to reassure oneself with the thought that history never repeats itself except as farce, and thus to justify our silence and our indifference. For my part, it is enough for me to know that this farce is sinister and stupid, in order to urge France to avoid this dishonour if there is still time.

For, on this continent and in this country, we know from lived experience that the poison of discrimination against the Other is an infernal machine that never stops, and certainly not with the first of its appointed victims. The monsters released by our time of transition and uncertainty, monsters that I already tried to warn against in *Dire non* [2014], are like a nest of Russian dolls that inure us to a cascade of other rejections, in an endless search for human inequalities and hierarchies: Roma, Gypsies and Tinkers, as ever; Jews, once again; blacks, still; homosexuals, too; even women, in a primitive return to anthropological inequality.

Just as clairvoyantly, Zola had a presentiment of this downward spiral. 'Today we persecute the Jews, tomorrow it will be the turn of the Protestants; and already the campaign is beginning,' he wrote in his *Lettre à la France*, published as a pamphlet on 7 January 1898, a few days before the famous *J'accuse…!* appeared in *L'Aurore*. And it was here that he added an observation that could well be true of today: 'The Republic is invaded by reactionaries of every kind, they worship it with a brutal and terrible love, they embrace it in order to stifle it.' It could not be better expressed.

The first intellectual and political expression of the modern far right, Action Française – founded by Charles Maurras in the wake of the Dreyfus affair – constantly undermined the Republic by opposing identity to equality, the passion for exclusion of the one to the emancipating liberty of the other. Casting four 'confederated estates', namely Jews, Protestants, foreigners and freemasons, outside the national community, Maurras called for a strong, vertical and hierarchical power, which he identified with the monarchy; while conceding that a perverted republic, under cover of personal and authoritarian power, could serve the same purpose.

'France, if you are not careful, you are heading for dictatorship,' Zola warned again in his *Lettre à la France*. And in his *Lettre à la jeunesse*, published a few weeks earlier on 14 December 1897, he appealed: 'Do not commit the crime of acclaiming a deception, of aligning yourselves with brute force, with the intolerance of fanatics and the voracity of the ambitious. At the end of that road lies dictatorship.'

As one evil follows another, hatred of human beings always ends up as rejection of democracy.

4

'Not all civilizations are of equal value,' a French government minister declared early in 2012, in the midst of the presidential election campaign. Some civilizations were 'more advanced', or 'superior' to others, and the minister went on to spell out that 'the question here is the Islamic religion.' A member of parliament retorted that this was the same 'insult to man' that lay at the root of those 'European ideologies that gave rise to the concentration camps'. This deputy, Serge Letchimy, saved our honour in the face of the disgraceful remarks of Claude Guéant.

There are times of national failure when you are ashamed not only of the leaders of your country, but also of a press that shores up their baseness with blind conformity and lack of conscience. The day after Letchimy's intervention in the Chamber of Deputies, where he was a Socialist representative for Martinique, we read in *Le Figaro* (in a front-page headline) and *Libération* (on p. 12, in the body of an article), the same word '*dérapage*' (outburst). The supposedly left-wing newspaper wrote that 'Deputy Letchimy's outburst cancels out Guéant's,' while the right-wing one reported:

'The outburst of a Socialist Party deputy has inflamed the campaign.'

This incendiary deputy was the political heir of the late Aimé Césaire, founder and leader of the Progressive Party of Martinique. And his 'outburst', which supposedly cancelled out the monstrosity uttered by Claude Guéant, itself reduced to a simple linguistic slip, had to be put down to 'attenuating circumstances' (again *Libération*), bound up, to quote Pierre Moscovici, director of the Socialist presidential campaign, with the 'sensitivities of a man from the Antilles'. Conflated with his origin, or even the skin colour that gives this away, Serge Letchimy was thus consigned to the category of emotiveness.

The situation was quite the contrary. The leading deputy for Martinique, who was also president of his regional executive, gave a reasoned speech argued with all necessary facts and references. Neither of the two press articles just mentioned quoted Serge Letchimy's full question to the prime minister, content simply to extract the words 'Nazism' and 'concentration camp' as if these were mere cries or insults shouted in the parliamentary chamber. We have to start therefore by acquainting ourselves with the Martinique deputy's argumentation. And this shows that he did no more than reiterate the principles on which European democratic values were founded in the wake of Nazi barbarity and the Jewish genocide.

In his question to the prime minister of the time, François Fillon, Serge Letchimy was actually addressing himself to Nicolas Sarkozy, who the day before – speaking to the right-wing extremists of the Union Nationale

Inter-universitaire – had hailed the apology for a hierarchy of civilizations by his interior minister, a particularly close colleague, as 'common sense'. It is necessary to emphasize that the ministers left the chamber when the speaker started to mention the 'dangerous and demagogic game' which aimed to 'win back on the terrain of the National Front' the 'shadowy France that cultivates nostalgia' for the colonial past. Let us also recall that this affront to parliament by the executive had no known precedent since 1898 – the very time of the Dreyfus affair, the opening scene in the emergence of the modern far right.

'No, Monsieur Guéant, it is not "common sense",' the deputy began, 'it is simply an insult to humanity. It is a denial of the wealth of human adventures. It is an assault on the harmony of peoples, cultures and civilizations. No civilization has a franchise on either darkness or august radiance. No people has the monopoly of beauty, the science of progress or intelligence. Montaigne said: "Every man bears the entire form of a human condition." I endorse this. But you, Monsieur Guéant, privilege the shadows. You take us back, day after day, to those European ideologies that gave rise to the concentration camps at the end of the long chain of slavery and colonialism. Was the Nazi regime, so committed to purification, civilization? Was the barbarism of slavery and colonialism a civilizing mission?'

Serge Letchimy was then cut off by the president of the National Assembly just as he started to invoke 'that other France, that of Montaigne, Condorcet, Voltaire, Césaire and many others, a France that invites us to recognize that every man …' And yet he had done nothing other than illustrate what this France had championed, the France that finally and belatedly triumphed in the political assertion that founds our Republic: the equality of human groups whatever their origin, race, belief, culture and civilization.

As an intellectual family, the modern far right asserted and constructed itself on the denial of this principle of equality. Whatever political party may be its embodiment, whatever its national variant or shade of radicalism, its founding creed is the rejection of equality and its political project the construction of a hierarchy. Or rather, the re-establishment of a hierarchy that it views as natural, in opposition to the republican philosophy of natural right. It advocates a hierarchy between nationalities, between citizens, between peoples, between nations, cultures, races, religions, etc.

And it is sure enough this creed to which the rise of a 'respectable' right under the presidency of Nicolas Sarkozy suddenly bestowed legitimacy, transforming it into acceptable opinion. It is this same creed that his chief collaborator, Claude Guéant, general secretary at the Elysée before becoming minister of the interior, promoted with deliberate provocation, going so far as to disqualify under the reproach of 'relativism' the republican ideal of equality – equality of rights, possibilities, liberties, humanities, etc. 'Contrary to what the relativist ideology of the left says, for us all civilizations are not of equal value' – that was the full sentence of the interior minister of the republican order, who became a minister of inhuman disorder.

Now we know in Europe, from the disastrous experience we have undergone, that this inegalitarian creed is potentially deadly. And if I insist on this, at the risk of repetition, it is because we do not repeat it often enough, given that those who could attest to it are no longer here to remind us. To hierarchize human groups and their creations (cultures, religions, civilizations) is to open the way to sorting and selection: to rejecting whatever is judged 'less advanced', selecting what is supposedly 'higher' and denying the humanity of what is deemed 'lower'. Of course, this is not a sufficient condition – there is fortunately still a long way to go from ideological blinkers to criminal policy – but it is a necessary one: accustomed to thinking in terms of higher civilizations, didn't the European peoples end up adjusting, with mute impotence or active readiness to oblige, to the crimes committed against the 'inferior' peoples they discriminated against?

That is why, under the immediate shock of the European catastrophe of the first half of the twentieth century, our Constitution (in the preamble of 1946, repeated in 1958) spelled out the meaning of the original proclamation contained in the 1789 Declaration of the Rights of Man. This stated that 'Men are born and remain free and equal in rights,' while the present Constitution adds: 'without distinction of race, religion or belief'. Equality therefore, still and again founded on the rejection of a hierarchical distinction between races, religions and beliefs – a list to which the 1958 version added 'origins', also spelling out that the Republic 'respects all beliefs'.

Equality as the creative principle of liberty and progress: the common right to possess rights, following the philosophy of natural right that shook the tyranny of monarchies based on a scale of privileges that divided humanity at birth. This is the democratic scandal which the anti-republican right, from its conservative heart to its fascist fringe, fought against so bitterly until triumphing under the Vichy regime.

It took the fall of Vichy along with the Nazi enormity to which it was allied, mountains of corpses, two world wars and countless crimes against humanity to force this right to accept the Republic, by way of the Gaullist revolt. And it is this conversion that Sarkozy and co. have undermined and corrupted, by stigmatizing one particular religion, Islam, and the Muslim culture associated with it, and so paving the way to the everyday persecution of a section of our compatriots, and thus contradicting the Republic. Re-forging the links made by the reactionary right of the interwar years, this 'respectable' right has legitimized the far right, taking up its xenophobic laments about those French men and women who 'because of uncontrolled immigration' no longer feel 'at home' (Claude Guéant, 17 March 2011), espousing its Islamophobic obsessions about the Islamic religion, 'the increase in the number of its adherents' being supposedly a 'problem' (Guéant again, on 4 April 2011).

It is very naïve of some people to reassure themselves by thinking that this was merely an electoral ploy. The fact is, they really mean it; Claude Guéant and his ilk are sincerely convinced of the enormities they utter. For, if the anti-Semitism that united them in the past has dissipated some-what under the weight of the European crime, there remains a matter on which the reactionary right still converges with the far right: the colonial question. This is the ghost that continues to prowl, from the closet of unappeased memories where it was buried in 1962 with the collapse of the colonial empire in Algeria – after an unjust and dirty war of denial of the rights of the Algerian people and of political abjection displayed in the general acceptance of torture.

If Serge Letchimy's reasoned question provoked such a fuss, it is because it struck precisely at this spot, where the future of France's relationship to the world is at stake, between identitarian retrenchment and national necrosis on the one hand, or, as we wish on the other hand, the truth of history and reconciliation with historic memory. The political hysteria that the deputy for Martinique received as his only reply is an admission that he had touched the nerve and spoken the truth. Far from uttering a crude enormity by associating the negation of the Other in the form of colonialism with the annihilation of the Other under Nazism, he did no more than recall France, our France, to a clear awareness of the criminal spiral that led to the European catastrophe.

In the wake of the Second World War, to see colonialism and Nazism as connected was a logical intellectual operation. It was necessary to understand how the unspeakable could have happened, this outbreak of barbarism at the heart of civilization. How could European societies have accepted their own criminal brutalization, how could their peoples have remained so largely indifferent to the destruction of the European Jews, how could their cultivated elites have accommodated to the racial discrimination that preceded this?

In 1951, in her pioneering book *The Origins of Totalitarianism*, Hannah Arendt placed the imperial expansion of colonial domination at the root of this European collapse into horror. She did not hesitate to discern in colonial domination, and in the 'scramble for Africa' in particular, 'many elements that, once brought together, would be capable of creating a totalitarian government based on race'. She even detected, in the combination of bureaucratic mechanism and wholesale massacre, one of the premises for the system of concentration camps.

The outrage of colonialism rebounded on Europe, producing within it civilized barbarians while it believed it was civilizing the barbarians outside its borders. As the historian Enzo Traverso has well demonstrated in his essay *The Origins of Nazi Violence*, subtitled in the French edition '*A European Genealogy*', the ideological ascendancy of biological racism ran parallel with the rise of the colonialism that it legitimized. From then on, he indicates, 'two complementary discourses were superimposed: the "civilizing mission" of Europe and the extinction of "inferior races", in other words, conquest by way of extermination.'

Recalling that the notion of '*Lebensraum*', far from being a Nazi invention, was a commonplace of European culture in the age of imperialism, with its higher civilizations and inferior races, Traverso describes 'the link attaching National Socialism to classical imperialism', its wellspring being the conviction that Europe 'was accomplishing a civilizing mission in Asia and Africa'. And he emphasizes that this link was obvious to the analysts of the 1930s and 40s. It is this obviousness that Serge Letchimy brandished

in the face of all ↙
century, allow it to b
level of government an
higher than others.

For want of a proper farev
it has reared up again with the
long contained. That the right su
of electoral tactics removes nothin_   ⌐;
it is a school of barbarism in our own ⌐   ⌐other
Martinique deputy, Aimé Césaire, said ↗   ⌐ly in the
1950s in his *Discourse on Colonialism*. Everyone famil-
iar with this famous text will have heard an echo of it in
Letchimy's intervention, as of the assertion of the connection between the crimes of colonialism and Hitlerism: what
Césaire called the 'formidable return shock' of the fatal
corruption that was colonialism, paving the way to Nazi
barbarism on the common terrain of a hierarchy of races
and civilizations.

Bringing in its wake financial greed and the brutalization
of societies, racial hatreds and pseudo-scientific theories
consecrating a superior West in the name of a 'civilizing
mission', the colonial adventure ended up de-civilizing
the colonized and making Europe itself a savage place.
'What am I leading up to?' asked Césaire in his *Discourse*,
prompted by the blithe assertion on the part of certain
French intellectuals of the 'unchallengeable superiority of
Western civilization'. 'To this idea', he replied,

that no colonization is innocent or carried out with
impunity; that a nation that colonizes, a civilization that

thus force – is already a sick
...ization morally affected, which irre-
a chain of consequences and denials, calls
...th its Hitler, in other words its punishment. Colonization is the bridgehead in a civilization of barbarism
which at any moment can lead to the negation of civilization pure and simple.

Serge Letchimy, by referring to those 'European ideologies that gave rise to the concentration camps at the end
of a long chain of slavery and colonialism', did no more
than continue Césaire, his political parent and that great
figure of whom it was said at the Panthéon, on 6 April 2011,
that with his death in 2008 'France lost one of the sons that
did it greatest honour.' Those words were pronounced by
Nicolas Sarkozy himself during a 'ceremony of solemn
homage of the nation' to Aimé Césaire, in a speech that celebrated this combatant who 'sought real equality of rights'.
If Claude Guéant had no memory of this, then no more had
the head of state, and if Sarkozy illustrates the barbarism
of supposedly higher civilizations, this is because for the
shadowy France embodied by this degraded right wing, the
only good anti-colonialism is a dead one.

Serge Letchimy is indeed alive, and his pillorying shows
us the path leading out of this national failure. He calls
on us to wake up in the same way that Césaire castigated
a Europe forgetful of itself, untrue to its own principles,
lacking respect for what it itself proclaimed. 'And this is the
great reproach that I address to this pseudo-humanism,'
wrote Césaire, 'that it has too long whittled away at human

rights, having in the past and still today a narrow and frag-
mentary conception of these, a partial one in both senses,
and at the end of the day, a sordidly racist one'.

The novelty of Sarkozy is to have asserted this without
any embarrassment, to have proclaimed these hierarchies
and theorized these inequalities, and thus to have led France
into a worrying regression vis-à-vis the world. By speaking
the language of barbarism. It is high time to counter him in
the authentic language of civilization.

5

In summer 2013, the Socialist government elected a year earlier met together for a seminar with an ambitious, not to say visionary agenda: where would France be in 2025, and what kind of France did we want by that date? Suddenly, politicians used to mistaking the urgent for the essential seemed to be tackling the urgency of the essential. They made an effort at last to look beyond the immediate. And for the space of a brief reflection, they abandoned the mere management of accounting imperatives and security bugbears to which their everyday ministerial activity had seemed to be reduced.

In the course of this government meeting, the then interior minister, Manuel Valls, who would become prime minister in 2014, explained the three challenges that, in his view, France would face over the next ten years. Here they are, in his own words, as summarized by the media: immigration, due to African demographics; the compatibility of Islam with democracy; and the problems raised by immigrant workers being joined by their families.

So, a year after we believed that a page had been turned

on Sarkozy's war of civilizations, this was the proposed agenda of a supposedly Socialist minister. From Claude Guéant to Manuel Valls, despite the change of party from an extreme-veering right to a right-veering left, we are thus faced with a continuity of xenophobic and, in particular, anti-Muslim obsession. It is no accident, then, if, between two evocations of immigration and foreigners, the rising star of the Socialist party should have pointed to a religion as such as a potential adversary of democracy.

Islam is used here to manufacture a global enemy. On the one hand, they threaten to invade us (immigration); on the other, they take advantage of our laws (family settlement); in both cases, they endanger our democracy. In the terms of the 'Muslim question', and by essentializing a religion, it is in fact the foreigner who is designated as the adversary, in a discourse which puts us on a war footing with the utmost casualness. A war against ourselves, against a section of our people, our history and our heritage.

The trouble is that this foreigner is not only outside, but also within. Among us, between us, one of us. Muslim, Arab, North African, immigrant, second-generation 'immigrant', but also worker, employee, neighbour; paying taxes, producing wealth, creating works of art, animating our cities, participating in the future of France … This part of ourselves is what such official speeches – irresistibly followed by acts, circulars, proclamations, decrees, laws, and the rest – train us to reject as foreign. In short, to exclude.

If these transgressions have not aroused more emotion on the left, this only signals how unable was the electoral change of 2012 to erect a solid barrier against the groundswell that had led the Sarkozy presidency into deep waters; how helpless to stop the increasingly commonplace injunction to our Muslim compatriots, in the wake of far-right propaganda, that they become invisible. That they wipe out any outward marker of their faith, minoritarian as it may be, whether in terms of clothing (the veil), food (halal) or place (the mosque).

Indeed, far from educating people firmly in the opposite sense, the new Socialist government let one of its members, the interior minister also responsible for religious affairs, to give the cue for a discourse that follows the same drift. Manuel Valls was not content to criticize the right of foreigners to vote in local elections (despite this being an election promise of François Hollande), to bury the proposed police acknowledgement form for stop-and-search (a question of routine discrimination against young people) and to assume presidential support in banning the Islamic scarf from public places (by criticizing a judicial decision by the appeal court). He added to these positions, which no right-wing minister would gainsay, the domestic exploitation of international tensions to construct a diabolical representation of Islam. He rejected, for example, the term 'Islamophobia', thus minimizing the discrimination that this denotes, by telling a lie about its supposedly Iranian origin, whereas its invention is well and truly French, dating back to 1910. 'Islamophobia is the Trojan horse of the Salafists,' he claimed in 2013. This explicit appeal to indifference backed by distrust – any who complain are potential terrorists – came on top of the invitation to wage civil war against those 'real enemies within' –

M. Valls again – the young French-born men and women who have strayed into radical Islamism.

Since taking office, Manuel Valls has in fact normalized that terrifying formula: the enemy within. An 'enemy within', he has publicly repeated on several occasions, locating this foe, more precisely, 'in our working-class neighbourhoods'. If these words still have any meaning, they mean that we have to prepare for war, a war of one France against another, a war that presupposes exceptions to the peaceful rules and customs of life in a democracy. A war against a religion (Islam) and against certain neighbourhoods (working-class): against a faith and a territory that are identified with a section of our most disadvantaged and unprotected compatriots.

These generalizations are not only stupid, they are above all dangerous. They illustrate a politics reduced to policing, and maintain the disastrous ideology that conditioned the United States' response to the attacks of 11 September 2001, a war of civilizations that, since the invasion of Iraq, has only aggravated the disturbances and rifts of the world bound up with the emergence of a political Islam. But, as shown by the calamity of the US Patriot Act, this legal power to act outside the law implies the infringement of basic liberties and a generalized surveillance. This kind of war, far from simply attacking the external adversary, violates the interior of a society itself.

The designation of scapegoats is inevitably accompanied by the development of state mechanisms to stigmatize, repress or repel these, which end up undermining democracy. It is by this process of habituation to discrimination, in which the politics of fear, though its own blindness, foments the upsurge of its enemies – their riots, their violence, their attacks, etc. – that the state of exception becomes the norm, to the detriment of the rule of law. Our indifference towards our Muslim compatriots is thus not merely a mistake in relation to them. It is also an offence to all of us, who risk, if we are not careful, losing a part of our freedoms.

In a democracy – an always incomplete ideal, in constant construction – the border between conservative, authoritarian and bellicose paralysis on the one hand, and totalitarian drift on the other, is never completely watertight. The work of Carl Schmitt, the pioneering theorist of the state of exception, attests to this, as does the itinerary of this German jurist himself, who moved from conservatism to Nazism. To proclaim the exception means first of all silencing any challenge: 'Sovereign is he who decides on the exception,' wrote Schmitt in his *Political Theology*, published in 1934, a year after Hitler came to power. It then means indicating to society an inexhaustible enemy, whose declared irregularity itself calls for an irregular response, outside norms and rules: 'With the exception, the force of real life breaks the carapace of a mechanism frozen in repetition.'

From this point on, fear becomes the argument of state power, setting society against itself in a fantasy of homogeneity and dragging it into an endless quest for scapegoats in which the Other, the different, the dissimilar, the dissonant, assumes the face of the foreigner, a foreignness both intimate and threatening. The adversary is then easily depicted as an internal enemy, an emblem of the alterity that must at all costs be suppressed or excluded, even annihilated by preventive counter-violence. It is enough to listen to the ordinary discourse of the war on so-called Islamist terrorism to hear the voice of this state of exception, which reduces politics to the police.

The comfort of security promised by the state is an illusion, into which democracy strays, gets lost, and perishes along with its vitality, its pluralism, its creative conflicts, its stimulating diversity, etc. The categorical imperative that the state uses as an 'open sesame' was explained early on by the philosopher Michel Foucault: 'Society must be defended.' In a double movement, by accustoming it to intolerance, measures to reduce its rights and freedoms are rendered tolerable, imposed on the pretext that society can no longer tolerate the very idea of a threat, a danger or a risk. And in this vicious spiral, Foucault continues, 'we see the appearance of a state racism: a racism that society will direct against itself, against its own elements and its own products. This is the internal racism of permanent purification, and it will become one of the basic dimensions of social normalization.'

Have we not seen, in recent public debates, the monstrous proposal of removal of nationality? The idea that there are some French people who are more so than others, and conversely, some who are French only under condition, on credit, in suspense? The vision, at the moment at least still symbolic, of one France that could deprive another, exclude it, cancel it, suppress it?

In June 2014, in the wake of the killing at the Jewish Museum in Brussels – the anti-Semitic crime of a young Frenchman back from the Syrian civil war – the president of the National Front hastened to relaunch this debate, without even knowing whether the killer had dual nationality. The next day, despite acknowledging that 'to be honest, this would not settle the underlying problem,' Manuel Valls, now in his role as prime minister, declared: 'We can deprive of their nationality those people who attack the fundamental interests of our country.' While accepting in this way the agenda of the far right, he admitted that he still did not know whether the murderer, born in Roubaix, had dual nationality. It turned out that he was French and French alone, born French into a family of Algerian origin, and the investigators have still not found, at the time I am writing these lines, proof of any other nationality.

When he was in opposition, Manuel Valls had refused to engage in this debate, sweeping away the subject with a single adjective: 'sickening'. That was in summer 2010, when Nicolas Sarkozy had exhumed it in a politician's forward flight to escape the moral discredit that was threatening him. In a sadly famous speech delivered in Grenoble, he did not hesitate to target 'criminals of foreign origin'. Scorning article 1 of the Constitution, which assures the 'equality before the law of all citizens without distinction of origin, race or religion', though as president of the Republic he is supposed to be its custodian, he proclaimed his intention to extend the scope of deprivation of nationality 'to any person of foreign origin who has deliberately carried out a life-threatening attack against a policeman, a gendarme or anyone possessing public authority'.

For the first time since the dark days of the Vichy regime, a policy of differentiation of French people according to their origin was thus officially proclaimed, from the mouth of the head of state. For a while, however, this crime against the Republic remained merely an aspiration; the envisaged measure of deprivation of nationality did not survive its examination by the French parliament in 2011, in the context of a projected law on 'immigration, integration, and nationality'. A number of parliamentarians, including some from the centre and right, fortunately remembered that, unless it was to deny its constitutional principles and, more fundamentally, the history of its own population, France could not create two categories of French citizens by distinguishing those who had acquired nationality from those who were born with it.

It remains that a terrifying step was taken, by floating the idea that it was possible, on the pretext of threats or dangers, not only to sort French people into categories, but to exclude some French people from France on the grounds of 'foreign origin'. Moreover, it is not accidental that this transgression, Sarkozy's speech in Grenoble, was accompanied by the stigmatizing of a particular population, the Roma, followed by their redefinition in ethnic terms.

The Roma are European in origin and Christian by religion. But they are poor, more than poor, poorer than the poorest, and this is the essential point on which everything turns and everything becomes explicable. That Roma and Muslims share the wretched privilege of being favourite targets of discrimination, in words and in actions, sheds light on the underlying question of the exacerbation of racism and xenophobia, the question that propagandists seek to spirit away and stifle, corrupt and dissolve, by proposing hatred and loathing in place of fraternity and solidarity. It is, quite simply, the social question.

We should remember that in 2013, Manuel Valls, once again, did not hesitate to place at the top of the national political agenda the Roma question – the Roma, rather than unemployment, living standards or education. According to him, 'populations of Roma origin' had no claim to remain in France because they 'have lifestyles that are very different from ours'. In other words, their way of being and living, their appearance, their culture, even their nature, make them unsusceptible to integration. At that point, unable to pass up such a great opportunity to air the traditional obsessions of his family of thought, Jean-Marie Le Pen insidiously slipped in: 'It may not be the most threatening immigration, but it is the most visible and smelly one.' Which the far-right weekly *Minute* translated into explicit language with its front-page headline: 'The Roma tree that hides the Arab forest'.

It is not just the customary Russian doll of racism that shows itself here, one scapegoat leading on to another. It is also how the social construction of a particular category, the poor among the poor, worthy of neither envy nor respect, is a propaedeutic to exclusion. Rejection of the poor and rejection of foreigners go hand in hand, as the German sociologist Georg Simmel remarkably understood. While the poor are clearly a part of society, the social order that they disturb or threaten constructs their exclusion. In this way, Simmel emphasized, the dominant prejudices make them 'undesirable', 'surplus' and 'useless'.

To construct the Roma into absolute foreigners, who, in

the term used both by Nicolas Sarkozy and Manuel Valls, do not have the 'vocation' to remain in France, is to habituate us to the idea of manufacturing and excluding other 'foreigners' who, albeit less poor, are no less undesirable. In this case, our compatriots of Islamic origin, culture or faith.

From Roma to Muslims, the ethnicizing of the social question, the reference solely to the origin, culture or faith of a section of the people, is a tool for getting rid of them. Of suppressing the disturbance to the established order. Of dissolving this into the deleterious passions of nation and identity. And of religion.

6

This is the point where the endless religious complaint against our Muslim compatriots comes into play. We want Muslims to be transparent. Self-effacing, secret, hidden. Assimilated, as we say in polite society. In actual fact, non-existent.

Assimilation is a terrifying injunction. It was also the demand of colonizers, and of the French in particular: the Other would be accepted only on condition that they ceased to be themselves, allowed to progress only if they agreed to resemble us, embraced only if they renounced everything that they were. This has nothing to do with the requirement of integration that expresses a quest for unity in plurality, a life to be constructed and invented together, by weaving bonds that are not those of destruction or distraction. The quest, in other words, for a life 'in connection', as defined so well by the poet Édouard Glissant: 'You exchange with the other without losing or denaturing yourself.'

The imperative of assimilation is a euphemism for disappearance. A way of desiring that the Muslims of France, in whatever degree they are Muslim, should no longer be so. Their religion is neither to be mentioned nor claimed, expressed nor practised. And this is how the sorcerer's apprentices who too often govern us give birth to monsters. For who cannot see this habituation to intolerance as making a silent call for the Muslims to no longer exist among us? The idea is that they should either rid us of themselves, or we should rid ourselves of them. That the varied humanity denoted by the words 'Muslim', 'Arab' or 'North African' should in future be somewhere outside and away.

This is why, in the project of negating a minority, initially denied of its rights before it is possibly denied its very existence, the question regularly waved in the way of a red rag is that of the visibility of Muslims in public space. Whether it is a matter of mosques, prayers, dress or food, these recurrent polemics, made up of media exaggerations in which a journalism of opinion flourishes rather than one of information, make France sick of itself. By this I mean France such as it is, such as it lives and works, such as it develops and changes. For they enjoin it to reject the pluralism that is its own characteristic, not to accept its own diversity and, as a consequence, not to face up to its social challenges.

In fact, the obsessional issue of the headscarf is a veil cast over our sensitivity, generosity and curiosity. To brandish the visibility of this piece of cloth as the key question for our public space is to encourage us to stop seeing the rest, everything that this focussing hides and obscures, and above all the social question, that of the working-class neighbourhoods. The religious hatred that an intolerant secularism expresses towards Islam and its practitioners is the expression of a social denial: a rejection of the dominated and oppressed whoever they may be.

This blindness is attested by the nonsense commonly spouted by those on the left who confuse religion and fundamentalism. More precisely, those who are quick to suspect newly arrived or recently established minority beliefs of religious fanaticism, despite these beliefs being shared by the new battalions of the working class who have arrived with their past and their culture, a wealth that constitutes both their distinction and their difference.

There is a phrase from Karl Marx on religion being 'the opium of the people' that is regularly wheeled out by propagandists of the secularism of exclusion to shut down debate, banning from public space any manifestation of religious adherence, any Muslim one in particular. Once we take the trouble to read it in context, we understand that Marx's message was quite different: not an invitation to make war on those who defend their beliefs, but an appeal to listen to the sufferings of which religion is the palliative, albeit an illusory one.

Here then is the passage from the 'Introduction to the Critique of Hegel's Philosophy of Right', a text of his youth published in 1844, in which Marx makes this comparison between religion and opium, understood as an artificial paradise and an illusory happiness: 'Religious distress is at the same time the expression of real distress and also the protest against real distress. Religion is the sigh of the oppressed creature, the heart of a heartless world, just as it is the spirit of spiritless conditions. It is the opium of the people.'

Having become famous, and cited as a verdict beyond appeal, this formula has been taken out of its historical context – that of the Western discovery of narcotic substances and the ensuing infatuation with them in high society. Opium here means an entertainment rather than a stupefaction, a pleasant means of dissipating a hateful reality, a way of repudiating it by the diversion of a virtual escape.

In short, these are not words of condemnation but of understanding, despite not indicating any complacency about religious ideas. But by refusing to reduce believers to a frozen identity, and wagering on their free will in the face of concrete experience, Marx deems what people do together more important than what they believe separately. He accepts them as they are, above all if, in the social exclusion in which they live, they have no other escape route than this religious sigh.

What Pierre Tévanian quite correctly refers to as the 'hatred of religion' that has seized hold of the left today, including the far left, makes it seem surprising that their intellectual reference points in the past criticized on the contrary the extremists of irreligion. Lenin, for example, denounced 'bourgeois anti-clericalism as a way of distracting the workers from socialism'. Rosa Luxemburg deplored 'the permanent war that has been waged for the last ten years against priests, [which] is for the French bourgeoisie one of the most effective ways of diverting the working class from social questions and stifling the class struggle'. And Leon Trotsky saw 'the abolition of chaos on earth', in other words an unlikely horizon, as the precondition for the suppression of its 'religious reflection'.

The same was true already at the time of the French Revolution. In 1792, Maximilien Robespierre appealed to the deity in his journal *Le Défenseur*: 'Oh God, this cause is thine.' And in 1793, Robespierre went on to attack the religious intolerance of those pursuing a radical campaign of de-Christianization. 'He did not want an atheist totalitarianism,' stressed the historian Henri Guillemin who, in 1989, on the occasion of the bicentenary of the French Revolution, published an excellent account of the Incorruptible's battle against a hatred of religion which, in truth, amounted to a fear of the populace, a great social fear, under the Voltairean veneer of enlightened thinking challenging the obscurantism identified with popular beliefs.

The title of Guillemin's essay was premonitory: '*Silence aux pauvres!*' In other words, may the poor surrender so that property is safe. And to that end, let us disqualify them by reference to their supposedly backward or fanatical superstitions, stripping them of their spiritual wealth and reducing them to being no more than arms that labour, and not also minds that dream. According to Guillemin, when Robespierre 'wished to express his full thinking on "the relation between religious ideas and republican principles", this time it was too much [for his opponents], as he exposed the docility towards despots of those whom he called the sect of the Encyclopaedia, provided those despots were enlightened.' This was the Robespierre – the bold Rousseauist whom the Voltaireans found insufferable – who chose Pentecost of 1794 to celebrate the Festival of the Supreme Being, by which action, according to Henri Guillemin, 'he signed his own death sentence.'

And if perchance revolutionaries scare you, whether Russian or French, there still remains Jean Jaurès, the tutelary figure of French socialism. Jaurès and his 'mental reservation', where transcendence has its part. Jaurès who proclaimed in the Chamber of Deputies in 1910: 'I am not among those frightened by the word "God".' Jaurès who, in his philosophy thesis 'The Reality of the Palpable World', championed the 'living infinity that is action'. Jaurès who, as deputy for Carmaux, expressed his metaphysical sensitivity in 1896 in the columns of *La Petite République*: 'I believe with a deep faith that human life has meaning, that the universe is a whole, that all its forces, all its elements, work together in a common plan and that the life of man cannot be isolated from the infinite in which it moves and towards which it tends.' Jaurès who would even write this challenge for the attention of strong and blasé minds: 'Every act of goodness is an intuition of truth, every effort in the cause of justice is God taking possession.' Jaurès whose progressive optimism did not shrink from appealing to Heaven: 'Justice, divine spark, sufficient to set every sun alight again'.

Beyond their differences of era and context, all these reminders send us the same warning: to agitate on the question of religion is a diversion from democratic and social issues. For those who resolutely take the side of the exploited, oppressed and dominated, it can never be the number one criterion. What we separately believe matters less than what we do together, our actions, our demands, our struggles, our solidarities. The scarf that a Muslim woman wears, the prayer that a worshipper repeats, the customs that a believer observes, all these choices which pertain to freedom of conscience matter less than the concrete involvement of the parties concerned in the things we have in common, in what we build together along our various paths.

To be a Muslim, to express or claim this, is thus no more incompatible in itself with the ideals of progress and emancipation than was the assertion by the workers and students of the Jeunesse Ouvrière Chrétienne and Jeunesse Étudiante Chrétienne of their Christian identity, at the time that they joined in the trade-union and political battles of the proletariat and of youth. Unless we take up once again colonial prejudices that essentialize other cultures in order to dominate and oppress them, reject or subject them, nothing justifies the allegation of incompatibility between the Republic, its ideals and its principles, and the demand to be recognized, respected and accepted as a Muslim.

Quite the contrary, since recognition of minorities is precisely a sign of the vitality of a democracy that accepts the diversity of its members, the plurality of their conditions and the wealth of their differences. A democracy that constructs in this way, through respect for these dissimilarities, a higher similarity, one proclaimed by the never exhausted, ever dynamic principles of liberty, equality and fraternity. If a synonym were needed for democracy, it would indeed be the word 'change': the rejection of predetermined lives, pre-assigned places, closed identities, and consequently immobile futures. A movement of encounter, exchange, surprise, in short, of relationship.

Beneath the Muslim question, therefore, there lies the French question: our capacity to reinvent a France that, instead of congealing into a fantasized and deadly sameness, launches itself towards the world by making its relationship to diversity the best key to every door.

7

The original Voltaireans at least accompanied the movement of a revolution, if only to curb its social and democratic ardours. Their epigones today, walled into their supposedly enlightened certainties, indifferent to the new contours and faces of the social question, simply mark time, content with their ignorance of the world and their lack of understanding of the Other.

In 1989, the year of the bicentenary of the Revolution, they had no qualms in speaking of capitulation, treason and destruction. Three resounding words as a declaration of war, in *Le Nouvel Observateur*, on a 'Munich of the republican school' – already on the subject of the Islamic headscarf. In 2014, some twenty-five years later, almost a generation, as if time had stood still, we find three of the protagonists from that time – the philosophers Élisabeth Badinter, Élisabeth de Fontenay and Catherine Kintzler – this time in *Marianne*, launching a new appeal, on the same wavelength if somewhat more moderate in expression: 'Secularism, it is time to stand up!'

The secularism they appeal to as a mantra, however,

has very little relation to the original secularism which, far from being a retrenchment against the assertion of minority religions, actually meant their recognition. Not their banishment into invisibility, but their right to public existence. Unfaithful to the promise of 1905, these modern secularists are to secularism what fundamentalism is to religion, or, if you prefer, what sectarianism is to politics. For the law of 1905, which separated the churches from the state, was far more a law of liberation, from any point of view, than one of prohibition or repression: the liberation of the Republic from a stand-off with the Roman Catholic Church; the liberation of Protestants and Jews, whose minority religions were finally recognized on the same basis as the majority religion; the liberation of citizens, invited to put aside their sectarian quarrels and focus on a far more promising agenda, that of democratic and social conquests.

The law of separation was a culmination more than a break, an old republican promise fulfilled at last with tact and intelligence, marking the end of a conflict rather than a relaunch, despite the horrified cries of the Roman Catholic ultras. It is too often forgotten that the separation was not the doing of Émile Combes, who was indeed the 'little father' of the 1902–03 battle against religious congregations, but rather of Aristide Briand, whose parliamentary success in this debate opened for him the way to power after his beginnings on the far left. Quite the contrary to Combes, Briand had no time for obsessive anticlericalism and chose a 'liberal separation', in the formula of the day, that is, one that respected freedom of conscience and worship.

Like many other republicans, who saw this as a treaty that would subject the church to the state, Combes was attached to the Napoleonic concordat of 1802. This was also the preference of Rome and the bishops, their reason being that Catholicism would thereby maintain its dominant and identitarian status, between a state religion and the religion of the majority of French people. 'You cannot wipe out fourteen centuries of history with a stroke of the pen,' Combes said as prime minister to the Chamber of Deputies on 26 January 1903, rejecting the very idea of separation. The law of 1905, choosing the plural in its very title, served as a response, and Briand never wavered in the debates, repeating quite correctly: 'We have in this country three churches,' meaning Catholic, Protestant and Jewish, to be treated with equal neutrality.

By 1905, however, Combes was no longer in power, and the concordat was no longer an issue. Late the previous year, the revelation of the *'affaire des fiches'* [affair of the files], the sectarian error of a war minister who relied on denunciations from Masonic sources in order to republicanize the army, proved fatal to the prime minister, who resigned in January 1905, putting an end to the longest-lasting ministry of the Bloc des Gauches. As for the Napoleonic concordat, this fell victim to a journalistic scoop, unearthed from the secrecy of ministerial offices and publicized by Jaurès himself, in the columns of a brand-new daily paper, his own, *L'Humanité*. On 17 May 1904, under the headline 'Provocation', Jaurès revealed the protest note from the Vatican against the visit to Rome of the president of the Republic, Émile Loubet, a note so insulting to

France that Georges Clemenceau had to outdo *L'Humanité* in *L'Aurore* the next day, under the eloquent headline 'The Pope's War'. The prompt recall of the ambassador was followed in July by a break in diplomatic relations between France and the Vatican, making separation inevitable.

Accelerating it, rather, as the mechanism was already well under way. The promise had figured ever since 1869 in all republican programmes, already admirably summed up by Victor Hugo in the National Assembly on 15 January 1850: 'The Church in its place and the State likewise'. But this was not simply the final stage in an old battle, it was above all a democratic achievement, a model of parliamentary work – complex, courteous and patient. From 1902 to 1903, no less than eight legislative proposals, representing a wide range of sensibilities, led the deputies to grasp the nettle and set up, in June 1903, a commission of thirty-three members. The Socialists, a minority within the Bloc des Gauches, then led the separatist campaign, acting as a spur to the majority and carrying with them the votes of the Radicals and Radical Socialists.

Four individuals were key to this: Ferdinand Buisson, the commission's president and a Radical Socialist, former editor-in-chief of the famous *Dictionnaire de pédagogie* under Jules Ferry, and recipient of the Nobel Peace Prize in 1927; Aristide Briand, the law's rapporteur, at this time a Jaurèsian Socialist who, after this masterstroke, would enjoy one of the longest ministerial careers of the Third Republic (serving as prime minister eleven times and more than twenty times as a minister, notably of foreign affairs), author in 1930 of the first memorandum on a European federal union, and also a recipient of the Nobel Peace Prize, in 1926; Francis de Pressensé, a Socialist deputy and ardent Dreyfusard who had become a close companion of Jaurès, president of the Ligue des Droits de l'Homme since 1904 and the author, in April 1903, of a draft law on the separation of church and state that would largely guide the work of the commission; and finally Jean Jaurès himself, whose personality as deputy for the Tarn then dominated parliamentary life by his intellectual strength and brilliant oratory, a man who was continuously taking risks and fighting, a man who definitively embodied a politics of speech in which speech is both act and will, and giving rise to a mystique, whatever an embittered Charles Péguy may have said of him.

The result was worthy of these four men: nothing less than a new and positive conception of secularism (*laïcité*), with no equivalent in other nations. This is laid down in the first two articles of the law, a model of clarity under the heading of 'Principles':

ARTICLE 1: The Republic guarantees freedom of conscience. It guarantees the freedom of religious worship, subject only to the restrictions laid down below in the interest of public order.

ARTICLE 2: The Republic neither recognizes, subsidizes nor pays salaries to any religious organization. As a consequence, from the 1 January that follows the promulgation of the present law, all budgets and expenses of the state, departments and communes pertaining to the practise of religious worship will be abolished.

The secular state was neither hostile nor indifferent to the various religions; it stood outside of them, its actions impinging on this world and no other, devoid of transcendence. The task that remained was to prevent the return of religion in other forms, such as political passions that sacralise nation, party, identity and so forth, those religions of earthly salvation that have caused as much destruction as have theocratic powers – a task that humanity has clearly not yet completed.

Even Péguy – turned away from Jaurès by Combism, that 'civilian Caesarism', and more generally by the Bloc des Gauches, and who, now converted to nationalism (*Notre patrie* was published in October 1905) would from now on constantly attack Jaurès in the meanest terms – had to agree: 'Like everyone else, I have to concur that this separation was effected more or less honestly, at least in the Chamber of Deputies ... it was in no way an exercise in persecution, a suppression of the Church by the State, or an attempt at oppression, anti-Catholic domination in the guise of anti-clericalism; it displayed a sincere effort at mutual liberation.'

True, the application of the law was not without tension or clumsiness, chiefly around the question of the inventories of religious properties before their devolution to voluntary associations, which required legislative adjustments through to 1908. But if the separation was a fruitful battleground for Action Française, contributing to anchor Catholic opinion in nationalism, it was not the crisis that had been feared. For the Catholic Church it was a beginning, an obligation to transform itself. For the Republic it was an end, the archiving of a painful affair.

In the closing debate in the Chamber of Deputies on 3 July 1905, Aristide Briand explicitly stated: 'The implementation of this reform will have the desirable effect of freeing our country from a genuine panic, under the influence of which it has greatly neglected so many other important questions, of an economic and social order, to which our concern for its grandeur and prosperity should already have imposed a solution.'

We find here an echo of the impatience of Jean Jaurès, challenging Prime Minister Combes a year earlier in the columns of *La Dépêche*:

> It is high time that the great but obsessive problem of the relations between Church and State be finally resolved, so that democracy can apply itself fully to the immense and difficult work of social reform and solidarity that the proletariat demand ... When the new session opens in October, the income tax must be discussed and voted. And in January the law on workers' pensions must be discussed and voted, and immediately after this vote, the debate on the separation of the churches and the state will commence.

In other words, room must be made for the social question. Room for the battle for all those social rights still pending, the eight-hour day, workers' pensions, the right to join unions, etc. Room – until summer 1914 – for the race between the social and the national, between the seemingly opposed logics of working-class internationalism and republican patriotism, a competition that would end with the dissolution of the former into the latter. In 1905, however, nothing was yet certain. Just as we hope that in 2014, nothing is yet settled in this similar race between identity and equality, between the exacerbation of the former and the extension of the latter.

'French democracy is not tired of movement, it is tired of immobility,' the young deputy Jean Jaurès proclaimed in 1887. Radically democratic and social, the movement that we champion here is a similar rejection of the immobility that deadens and corrupts. And, just as pages are held together by their edges, so the fate we reserve for minorities who are still on the borders of the city will determine the outcome. The result for all those who do not have the same beliefs as the majority, those who claim their difference, those not content with thinking differently but who see themselves as different. Yesterday Protestants and Jews, today Muslims.

8

In every country, the lot of minorities speaks of a society's moral state. In writing the present book, therefore, my concern is for the Muslims of France. I have no doubt that elsewhere, in countries where the dominant culture is Muslim, there is cause to write in defence of other minorities: Christians, Jews, agnostics, animists, those without religion, unbelievers, or even minorities arising from Islam itself – Shias in the Sunni countries, and vice versa. Beyond the bounds of my own land, therefore, I am also writing against that war of the worlds into which a few seek to drag nations, by manufacturing identity-based hatreds for which religion serves as an alibi.

But I am in France, I live and work here, and it is here too that this awakening of consciences is needed. Never can crimes committed by those so-called Muslims who have themselves stumbled into these endless wars justify our persecution of the Muslims of France in return. Never can individual madness or distant conflicts authorize us, in our country, to equate men, women and children en bloc with a peril that supposedly threatens our integrity, the very purity of our national community, on the pretext of their faith, their beliefs, their religion, their origin, their culture, their appearance or their allegiance.

The disorders of the world can never excuse our forgetting the world. Its complexity, its diversity and its fragility. It is enough to look back on the last four decades, starting from the catastrophic results of actions in the Middle East and around the Mediterranean by states that claim to be Western, since the time that political Islam arose in 1979 with the Iranian revolution, to take the measure of the disastrous consequences of this blindness. While the Palestinian question remains intolerably unresolved, despite the recognition of the state of Israel by the majority components of the Palestinian national movement, Europeans and North Americans have continued to support, alternately or in parallel, dictatorial secular states or obscurantist religious regimes which, beneath their differences, display a common indifference to the rights of their peoples.

Now, starting with the Tunisian uprising in December 2010, these peoples have finally decided, in a geopolitical shock wave without borders, to make their rights prevail. By starting to write their own history once again, they have given the lie to prejudices, our own in particular, that condemned them to be subject to authoritarian regimes or enclosed in religious extremism. Suddenly we discovered peoples inspired by ideals of democracy, liberty and justice, peoples who shared the same hopes as ourselves, dreams of emancipation and desires for movement.

It is this history that has since been written, inventively and generously, chaotically or dramatically, from

Tunisia to Egypt, from Syria to Yemen. That the event was unpredictable is precisely its first virtue: it has shaken what seemed unshakeable, reversed what was immobile and destabilized what appeared immutable. This is certainly what in history is called a revolution: not something foreseen or controlled, but something that erupts without warning and invents its own path, without a pre-established programme, party or leader, with advances and setbacks, hopes and disappointments.

Whether it succeeds or fails, whether it is crushed or confiscated, is clearly a different matter and depends on the balance of forces, as well as on other peoples in the world who are themselves actors, according to whether they are indifferent or show solidarity. Because these revolutionary events, in their clear uncertainty and great disparity, have nonetheless offered an unexpected chance to shake off a double constraint: on the one hand, that which imprisons peoples in misfortune and oppression, denial of justice and rights, and on the other hand, that which immures the rest of the world in the fear of extremist disorders born from this suffering. The fear of threats that are themselves invoked to justify the indefinite continuation of injustices and inequalities, symbolized by the sorry fate inflicted on the Palestinian people.

The game is not over: witness the Syrian civil war and the military regression in Egypt, as against the cautious advances of the Tunisian democratic revolution. God or Army, barbarism or dictatorship, denial of democracy in each case ... The return of this vice in which peoples who freed themselves have once more been trapped threatens

our own public debate. It debases and maddens it, undermining the hope of a new Mediterranean era that could
potentially free us, in France itself, from the negative
passions on which the post-9/11 politics of fear based
its success, dragooning our societies into an endless war
against a terrorism identified with Islam.

The ideologists of the clash of civilizations, who essentialize identities, cultures and religions, cannot cope with
the uncertainties and precautions that a grasp of this multi-
form crisis requires, a crisis in which democratic upsurges
occur side by side with bloody calamities. Quick to decree
that Islam is incompatible with democracy, these firebrands
for the war of the worlds have wagered from the start on
the defeat of peoples who should rather be supported in
their demands for the universal ideals of liberty and equality. All the more so because their insurgency attests to the
profound evolution of their societies, converging far more
than diverging from our own – demographically, culturally, and in terms of the family – as was so comprehensively
shown in 2007 by Youssef Courbage and Emmanuel Todd
in *A Convergence of Civilizations*.

The champions of the politics that accompanied the dis-
asters of the post-9/11 period have therefore had constantly
to return to their obsessions – xenophobic, discrimina-
tory, essentialist – closing with unconcealed pleasure the
gateway of hope opened in 2011. In so doing they compro-
mise our own future, given how greatly this depends on a
relationship with the other Mediterranean nations, for clear
enough geopolitical reasons in which history, geography,
economics, demography and culture are all involved. And

this is why the Muslim question holds the immediate key to our relation to the world and to others, for France and indeed for Europe as a whole.

In an essay entitled 'Islam as News', a concrete illustration of his reflections on Orientalism as the construction of an imaginary East by the West, Edward Said long ago identified this exception of the Muslim question as the latest blind spot in our relation to the Other, the different, the dissonant and the unlike: 'Malicious generalizations about Islam have become the last acceptable form of denigration of foreign culture in the West; what is said about the Muslim mind, or character, or religion, or culture as a whole cannot now be said in mainstream discussion about Africans, Jews, other Orientals, or Asians,' he wrote in the preface to the 1997 edition of *Covering Islam*.

A Palestinian who lived in the United States, politically liberal in the Anglo-Saxon sense of democratic radicalism, Edward Said, who died in 2003, could hardly be suspected of sympathy for the conservative and reactionary forces of the Muslim world, emphasizing as he did in the same text the 'impassioned climate' that these foment and the 'unappealing image of Islam' that they convey. But what struck Said, in New York where he was living and from where he sounded this alarm four years before 11 September 2001, was the instrumentalization in our countries of the 'label "Islam"' as 'a form of offensive', along the lines 'fundamentalism equals Islam equals everything-we-must-now-fight-against, as we did with communism during the Cold War.'

Criticizing the 'unacceptable and irresponsible generalizations' in which 'concrete circumstances are obliterated,'

Said argued that so-called '"Islam" defines a relatively small proportion of what actually takes place in the Islamic world, which numbers a billion people, and includes dozens of countries, societies, traditions, languages, and, of course, an infinite number of different experiences. It is simply false to try to trace all this back to something called "Islam",' as if 'Islam regulated Islamic societies from top to bottom, that *dar al-Islam* is a single, coherent entity, that church and state are really one in Islam, and so forth.' What worried Said were the consequences of this Western blindness. Most particularly, that it produces, in a kind of self-fulfilling prophecy, 'an "Islam" fully ready to play the role prepared for it by reaction, orthodoxy, and desperation'.

Said's gloomy prediction has sadly been realized, radicalizing still further, if this were possible, the dominant Western representations of Muslims. And what has happened in the Egyptian, Syrian, Iraqi, etc. crises, depending on their outcome, has confirmed or refuted this caricature that fuels identitarian and xenophobic retrenchment in both East and West. But if our ability to influence this course of events is minimal indeed, our responsibility is all the greater for its effects closest to home, in France, the European country with the largest Muslim community in the varied meaning of this adjective – origin, culture, religion – and where Islam is the largest minority religion in relation to Catholicism, above Judaism and Protestantism.

The historian Lucette Valensi also offers us a warning, based on the long historical presence of Muslims in Europe, in her book *Ces étrangers familiers*. She particularly cautions against the trap of a supposedly 'Judeo-Christian foundation' of European civilization, which by the same token excludes its other components and makes us forget how Christians themselves slaughtered one another in the name of religion. 'When some people attribute to Europe a Christian foundation', she writes, 'and at the same time assign to it a singular role in the destiny of the world, other civilizations are pushed out of sight, while at the same time non-Christian citizens of contemporary Europe are denied this role. The true Europeans are the Christians, others are just guests and must remain so.'

Valensi thus unmasks the 'fallacious co-option' that draws the Jews, whom Europeans persecuted for so long, into this essentialism of a Europe that excludes above all Muslims, but also relegates to second-class status the descendants of Chinese, Hindus or Africans who do not have a monotheist religion. 'To appear more generous', she continues, 'or perhaps because we have finally accepted the Jewish presence, or again because we remember from time to time how we sought to obliterate this, an extra adjective is introduced: the European tradition is now Judeo-Christian.'

Looked at in historical terms, however, this is a fiction that conceals a 'double operation': on the one hand, to recover 'the illusion of a still universal vocation', at a time when Europe is no longer alone in setting the tone of the world; on the other, to comfort 'the illusion of preserving a homogeneous identity inherited from the distant past, when this long-term purity is in no way verifiable'.

At the end of the day, the historian concludes, this ideological construction 'consists in erecting an unbridgeable external border, excluding every country and nation that does not share this Christian past; and drawing an internal border in relation to those inhabitants of Europe who are not fully convertible into European citizens because they originate from these non-Christian lands'.

This operation mutilates and betrays us, promoting a Europe forgetful of itself, of the diversity that has shaped it and the exclusions that have wounded it. To defend the right of European Islam to recognition is on the contrary to be faithful to the best of the European legacy, made up of a diversity of languages, religions and origins, of individual freedom and social tolerance.

9

'For the first time, the Other is truly becoming a problem internal to European culture, a moral problem concerning each one of us.'

These words were penned by a European journalist, and no ordinary one at that. They are the words of a great reporter who crisscrossed the whole world in a life spent on voyages of generous discovery, precisely of other peoples, other individuals, other cultures, particularly in Africa. The words of a Polish citizen, born in 1932, who could not forget that his land was chosen by the Nazis as the territory for their extermination camps, permanently marked by the massacre of men, women and children for the crime of having been born as Others – Jews, Gypsies, etc.

The book from where I have taken these words is entitled *The Other*, and serves as a testament, a legacy to future generations. Ryszard Kapuściński published it the year before his death in Warsaw in January 2007. In a compilation of several lectures, he here transforms his professional experience into political reflection. From the ever uncertain path of true reportage, where 'each encounter with the Other is an enigma, an unknown, even a mystery,' he learned that 'we are responsible for the journey that we make.' In other words, this Other, the encounter with whom is surprising, disturbing or bewildering to us, decisively depends on ourselves. On our approach, our gaze, our curiosity. On our 'goodwill towards them', he sums up. Our refusal to go along with 'the indifference that creates a climate that could potentially lead to Auschwitz'.

'Stop! Look!' Kapuściński exclaims to his reader, in a section celebrating the thought of the philosopher Emmanuel Lévinas. 'Beside you, the Other is to be found. Go to meet him. The meeting is the test, the most important experience. Look at the face that the Other offers you! By way of this face, he conveys to you his own person, still better, he brings you closer to God.'

The coldness, insensitivity and ignorance that lead to a neglect of the Other are so many steps that take us away from the good, while the discovery of their difference, 'this alterity that is a treasure and a value', draws us towards good.

But such an approach is not automatic; it implies an effort, and Kapuściński actually writes of 'a gift of self and heroism'. For we have to think against ourselves, our habits, our inheritance, against the five centuries during which Europe dominated the world, politically, economically and culturally, forming relationships with the Other that were deeply asymmetrical, dominating, paternalist. We are now living a kind of return to sender in which the Other definitively invites himself to the banquet of the world, even while our own continent, Europe, can no longer pretend to 'reign exclusively, sheltered from any threat, autocratically as it had done hitherto'.

This is the great challenge that awaits us, to which we are summoned and for which we will be judged, according to whether we treat the Other as a brother or as an outsider. This Other who, in our societies, has taken the shape of a Muslim. This Other on whose fate depends our own relationship to the world. Our adversary is nothing more than fear, and we have to oppose it with courage, a courage which by example awakens trust – the courage of principles, of boldness, of resistance, of dignity, of solidarity.

Yesterday as today, fear of the world is always the wellspring of xenophobia and racism. Unable to rise to the challenges of the world, to understand them or control them, the rulers who trade in these hatreds seek to survive by designating scapegoats, in an effort to free themselves from the fear that inhabits and paralyses them.

'He is a man who is afraid,' Jean-Paul Sartre wrote of the anti-Semite in 1946, in his *Anti-Semite and Jew*. But the portrait still holds good for all those today who hate Jews, black people or Gypsies:

He is a man who is afraid. Not of Jews, to be sure, but of himself, of his consciousness, of his liberty, of his instincts, of his responsibilities, of solitariness, of change, of society, and of the world – of everything except the Jews … The Jew only serves him as a pretext; elsewhere his counterpart will make use of the Negro or the man of yellow skin. The existence of the Jew merely permits the anti-Semite to stifle his anxieties at their inception by persuading himself that his place in the world has been marked out in advance, that it awaits him, and that tradition gives him the right to occupy it. Anti-Semitism, in short, is fear of the human condition.

Sartre's reflections flushed out at an early date what has always been the nub of the French mental block, and that it is high time to undo: the refusal to accept the Other as such, the compulsion to assimilate him to oneself, this abstract universal that only accepts the Jew, the black or the Arab on condition that they divest themselves of their history and their memory. Sartre, for example, mocks as a false friend of the Jews a 'democrat' who 'reproaches [the Jew] with wilfully *considering himself* a Jew', while the anti-Semite 'reproaches the Jew with *being* Jewish'. '[The democrat] recognizes neither Jew, nor Arab, nor Negro, nor bourgeois, nor worker, but only man – man always the same in all times and all places,' and in this way misses the singular: 'by individual he means the incarnation in a single example of the universal traits which make up human nature.'

This is precisely what our Muslim compatriots experience, having for so long been simultaneously consigned to their origin and prevented from claiming it. Ethnicized and stigmatized at once. Reduced to a univocal identity in which their own diversity and the plurality of their allegiances is obliterated, and rejected as soon as they try to assume this by proclaiming themselves for what they are.

We are here at the heart of a challenge to France that has too long been held in suspense: the challenge to finally learn to think at the same time the universal and the singular, solidarity and diversity, unity and plurality. And as a result, to firmly reject the neo-colonial demand to assimilate that seeks to compel one section of our compatriots (of Islamic culture, Arab origin, black skin, etc.) to erase themselves and dissolve, in short, to whiten themselves. The requirement, in other words, to disappear in order to be accepted.

The knot in which France today is tied, and that we all have to untie together, is this nostalgia for a model of integration that was indeed tremendously effective, but could only work in a relationship of dissymmetry between the strong and the weak. It was the model of a 'truly great' France whose colonial empire assured it a relation to the world that it believed to be stable and permanent, if not immutable. Diversity here seemed to have its place, yet only as a diversity dominated and oppressed, recognized or celebrated, but either way folkloric. However, in the absence of the emancipation of genuine equality, this visibility was no more than a side effect of power, whether in the form of assimilationist promotion or fraternal solidarity. The Other was only recognized as such depending on the goodwill of the dominator, and only insofar as he submitted to this.

In the more than half a century since this illusion evaporated in the violent rift of the colonial wars it gave rise to, France – at least the France of its political, economic and academic elites – has not managed to accept our nation as it has become, as it lives and works, as it grows and expands. Rather than lighting beacons to point out the future we have to invent, those who govern us can only look in the rear-view mirror at a consummated past. When they hear the word 'multiculturalism', which is no more than a statement of France's diversity and the wealth of relationships that this enables, they fear a supposedly destructive 'communitarianism' against which they raise, with crazed urgency, the shield of a rigidified secularism, unfaithful to its original meaning.

It is not enough to oppose instances of Islamophobic, racist, xenophobic violence case by case. We must counter it with a competing imaginary, a creative and mobilizing one that uplifts and liberates. This alternative imaginary was superbly defined again by Jean-Paul Sartre, in that vigorous investigation of our silences, forgetting and blindness that constitutes his *Anti-Semite and Jew*, written in the wake of the catastrophe of genocide:

> What we propose here is a concrete liberalism. By that we mean that all persons who through their work collaborate toward the greatness of a country have the full rights of citizens of that country. What gives them this right is not the possession of a problematical and abstract 'human nature', but their active participation in the life of the society. This means, then, that the Jews – and likewise the Arabs and the Negroes – from the moment that they are participants in the national enterprise, have a right in that enterprise; they are citizens. But they have these rights as Jews, Negroes, Arabs – that is, as concrete persons.

More than half a century has passed, and this perspective of
reconciliation with ourselves, our people and its diversity,
is still remote: the arduous and painful victory won by our
Jewish compatriots – to be accepted as both Frenchmen *and*
Jews – by the necessary detour of an awakening of memory
and historical truth remains to be permanently won for our
Muslim, Arab and black compatriots. The truth of history,
the reconciliation of memories: who cannot see how this
path, accepted for the Jews of France, has yet to be taken
clearly and with determination by our leaders when it is a
matter of other wounds of our history, our blindness and
colonial crimes, and the victims that attest to these failings?

Time is running out. Faced with the triple crisis – democratic, economic, social – that is undermining our country,
a far right has arisen, the back-up to an 'official' right wing
that has stubbornly chosen the path of division, pitting
France against itself in a war of identities, origins, religions, and the rest. The oligarchy that has presided over
thirty years of deregulation and financialization wants to
stop the poor (in other words, all those less rich than themselves) from rocking the boat by pitting them against one
another, rather than realizing what they have in common
– their social condition, their employment situation, their
shared community, their living conditions, and much more.

This is certainly why the Sarkozy administration constantly spread the ideological poison of the inequality of
peoples and the hierarchy of cultures: from the abortive
debate on national identity, to the Grenoble speech sin-
gling out French citizens of foreign origin, by way of the
praise of 'superior' civilizations, not forgetting increasingly

repressive and unjust policies on migration or the stigmatizing of all those, such as the European Roma, who refuse
to be assigned to a unique identity or place.

These were not just words: they released a tremendous
violence that was not merely symbolic. And, far from
abating with the change of president in 2012, this violence
has continued to grow, encouraged by the inaction of a state
itself pervaded by fear of the unknown and the unfamiliar,
unable to countenance the new imaginary that we need, let
alone to state it and defend it. All those women and men
that this violence targets and singles out, by reason of their
origin, their appearance or their religion, live and experience it in their bodies and in their souls. Are we going to
leave them to deal with it alone, as though it were a matter
of individual sensitivity and not of collective principles?
Will we remain indifferent to the resurgence, no longer
at the periphery of public debate but at its centre, of the
deadly ideologies of yesterday, this barbarism concealed
in the pathological delirium of civilizations that have lost
their way? Will we remain silent?

In *Causes communes*, a recent essay on the solidarity established between Jews and blacks around a shared awareness
of the persecutions they faced, the socio-anthropologist
Nicole Lapierre drew attention to what could be a real new
awakening, that of a concrete humanism eschewing uni-
formization or trivialization; that of empathy. Empathy,
she says, is 'the capacity to adopt and understand the point
of view of another person, to conceive their experience,
their thought, their feelings, without however fusing or
confusing oneself with them'. A concrete humanism, she

emphasizes, that 'goes against the old and hateful recipe of insecure governments that consists in stigmatizing populations or setting them against one another in order to create a diversion or to serve as an outlet for frustration. Blacks against Jews, Christians against Muslims, settled people against travellers, or others again, it scarcely matters who they are in this dangerous game of fools.'

To illustrate this courageous path, Lapierre quotes the novelist André Schwarz-Bart, who portrayed the persecution of Jews in *The Last of the Just*, and then of black people in *A Woman Named Solitude*; a writer who appealed to 'the power that the I has to say Thou'. This is echoed in the life's work of Frantz Fanon, a West Indian from Martinique and a soldier with Free France, who embraced the cause of Algerian independence and drew from it his great outcry, *The Wretched of the Earth*, speaking for all the peoples of the Third World struggling to regain their sovereignty. Fanon, committed to the emancipation of those still officially labelled 'French Muslims of Algeria', but who nevertheless combatted any confinement of a person to their origin: 'No one should try to fix man, as his destiny is to be released.' Fanon, who presciently warned against competitive victimhood and the necrosis of memories, who rejected being a slave to the enslavement of his ancestors while seeking to connect all discriminations together: 'An anti-Semite is necessarily anti-black.'

Fanon, then, who in the last lines of his first book, *Black Skin, White Masks*, floated a question whose echo still reverberates through the present time:

Superiority? Inferiority?

Why not simply try to touch the other, feel the other,
discover each other?

Was my freedom not given me to build the world of
you, man?

At the end of this book we would like the reader to feel
with us the open dimension of every consciousness.

My final prayer:

O my body, always make me a man who questions!

This is the road we must once again take, find and reinvent.

10

Our empathy has been wanting for far too long. Empathy with Muslims, with Arabs, with Jews, with blacks, with Roma and Gypsies. With all those who, successively or at the same time, fall victim to this barbaric ideology of self-proclaimed higher civilizations versus those accursed peoples who once more prowl among us. It is in hopes of making up for this delay that I have sought to oppose this here with the experience of the world, of diversity and pluralism, that has made French men and women of us.

I am one among millions of others, and I have no better claim than that to justify this book. I speak as a Frenchman who does not reduce himself to his origin. Born in Brittany to Breton parents, one of them raised a Catholic, the other a Protestant, I was not myself baptized. I grew up far from metropolitan France until the age of eighteen, first in Martinique and then in Algeria (after independence); these were the true countries of my childhood and adolescence, the homelands of my youth.

I have thus been shaped by a variety of cultures (Breton, French West Indian, Creole, Caribbean, North African,

Arab, Berber, French ...), in which different spiritual influences come into play (Catholicism, Protestantism, voodoo or *quimbois*, Islam ...), including that of diaspora Judaism, to which I am linked through my partner, whose origins lie in the Jewish emigration from central Europe. Not counting, to be sure, the republican schooling imparted by my parents, who were deeply attached to the French system of secular education.

To sum up, I am non-religious, with no taste for transcendence but without an unhealthy obsession about those for whom this matters. Especially given that my generation, born after the global catastrophes of the first half of the twentieth century, has learned that civilizations which appeal to reason, or even to a rejection of God, can just as well succumb to a collective unreason that leads them to commit horrific acts of criminal insanity.

My only concern therefore is with the immediate domain that lies wholly within our remit, which is the present, regardless of whether one believes in an afterlife: this common world that we have to construct all together, rather than destroy by sliding back into a war of all against all. A world that is fragile and uncertain, and whose secret divinities are beauty and goodness. It is in their name that we must say no to the approaching shadow, by a show of concrete solidarity with the women and men it most threatens. And in first place among these are our compatriots of Islamic origin, culture or belief.

In April 1941, when night had descended upon Europe, the poet Aimé Césaire, born in Fort-de-France, wrote the following words in the first issue of his magazine *Tropiques*:

Everywhere we look, darkness is winning. The fires are going out one after another. The circle of shadow is tightening, amid the shouts of men and the cries of wild beasts. And yet we are among those who say no to the shadow. We know that the salvation of the world depends on us as well. That the earth needs every one of its sons, including the most humble. The Shadow is winning … 'Ah, all our hopes are not too much, if we are to look the century in the face!' Men of goodwill can bring a new light to the world.

Men and women of goodwill, what are we waiting for?

Postscript

A Letter to France

There are tests that reveal a nation to itself. Since the terrorist attacks in Paris on 7, 8 and 9 January 2015, everyone in our country of France has been faced with such a test. Will we prove able to recognize the France that exists, lives and works, suffers and strains, invents and dreams itself, stands up and comes together? Or will we remain blind to it while denigrating and disparaging it? To demean and madden it by dragging it into this panicked self-hatred, rife with unhappy questions of identity, French suicide and imagined submission, in which bitterness and resentment fester?

The true face of France is that of the women and men who died in these three days of assault on our freedoms. Three days of crime against a magazine, the killing of policemen and the murder of Jews. An assassination of the right to live, think and express oneself safely, in the diversity of our opinions and our origins, our convictions and our beliefs. Those who were killed by the three terrorists were the very image of our country: Christians, Jews,

Muslims, freemasons, atheists, agnostics, born here and elsewhere. Motley and plural, of many cultures and faiths, from near and far away. A nation nourished by a constant dialogue with the world, in which identities are invented in the fabric of relationships, exchanges and sharing that is the foundation of common causes.

In this test, that was the face of our France, without borders or walls. The face evoked by the words of the 'Internationale,' the song of Paris proletarians which, after so long making the rounds of the world, accompanied the coffin of Charb, the editor of *Charlie Hebdo*, at his funeral in Pontoise. 'The human race ... no saviours from on high ... our own right hands ... the common weal ... the earth belongs to men ... equality wants other laws.' Humanity as a common demand, with no distinction of origin, appearance or belief, in mutual respect for our differences of heritage and belonging.

In a sign of destiny, this true portrait of France, selfless and valiant, hard-working and bold, was embodied by a man who lacked French nationality before the miracle of his gesture bestowed it on him. This is the young man who rescued the hostages in the kosher supermarket: Malian by origin, Muslim by belief, an immigrant worker, yesterday threatened with expulsion, today a citizen with full rights ... As if the world had suddenly come to our aid. A world which has for centuries made France, shaped its people, contributed to its wealth.

A Muslim hero, then. And there were two others, Muslim by culture or belief, among the dead at *Charlie Hebdo* – a proof-reader and a policeman, a guardian of language and a guardian of the peace. Of the French language, of French peace. If I underline this fact, it is certainly not to distinguish them from the other victims, but simply to utter this simple truth: Islam belongs to France, as Angela Merkel said about her own country, Germany, in the face of racist demonstrators who call for a Europe without Muslims, amputated of a part of itself, rid of a part of its humanity.

This truth needs to be spoken aloud, now more than ever. Already mistreated, it is now threatened. First of all by terrorists, who always bank on exacerbating the situation, on a *politique du pire*. By the deeds of these three murderers, and by the mad and deadly ideology that armed them. By the gravity of crimes committed in the name of a religion, Islam, despite the fact that they betrayed and disfigured this religion, caricaturing it more savagely and painfully than any printed cartoon, inoffensive and innocent. In sum, by this denial of their own humanity in the form of a cold and premeditated murder of other human beings because of their ideas, their origins or their beliefs.

Faced with the spectacle of their actions, for which they were accountable and paid with their lives, we might recall the words of Charles Péguy – a Christian republican, uncomfortable on both counts – about the 'devout party', meaning religious sectarians of every sort: 'Because they lack the courage to exist in the world, they believe they are from God. Because they lack the courage to be a party of man among others, they believe they are the party of God. Because they love no one, they believe that they love God.' 'But Jesus Christ himself was human,' Péguy retorted, and the same could be said of Moses or Mohamed.

'It is not enough to vilify the temporal in order to elevate oneself into the category of the eternal … It is not enough to vilify the world to rise into the category of God … No one should be diminished so that others may appear greater,' added the Dreyfusard Péguy in his inimitable style, in which prose and homily combine. These lines were written a few weeks before he went to his death, on 5 September 1914, as Europe was collapsing blindly into an endless war of nations and civilizations, down to the final barbarism of a crime against humanity. Even though on its centenary in 2014 we clearly remembered that tragic error, with its *unions sacrées* and propaganda of deceit, can we now avoid its repetition between East and West?

Put in this way, the question is not alarmist, simply lucid. The context may well be very different, but we know from recent international experience the trap being laid for us. The trap of a politics of fear which, blind to causes in striking against effects alone, merely compounds the dangers and threats. Today we are paying the price for the dramatically misguided reactions of the United States after 11 September 2001: not only with the emblematic moral discredit of a democracy that undermined its own basic freedoms and human rights to the point of justifying torture, but above all after the strategic mistake of the invasion of Iraq fertilized fresh ground for totalitarian ideologies, of which the Islamic State is now the standard-bearer as it proceeds to the deadly destruction of that country and its institutions.

This warning is motivated by concern for France, its security and its welfare. In the face of disturbances born of injustice and poverty, resentment and humiliation, politicians without stature reach for authoritarian and security-oriented fixes, hastening to proclaim that these will put an end to the disturbance, even at the cost of new injustices. Short-sighted and short-termist, such gestures solve nothing fundamental and only build a temporary protection behind which the same causes produce the same effects, enabling the enemies of democracy and freedom to find new arguments and new recruits.

Responsible politicians, on the other hand, always seek to identify the injustice that is the cause of disorder, with the aim of understanding, reducing and resolving it. They evince a genuine concern for the safety of their people and, more broadly, of humanity. It is crucial to take this risk of inviting reflection beyond emotion and, consequently, to understand that the totalitarian violence that has struck us will not only not cease but will worsen if we fail to rise to the measure of the challenge: to confront the injustice, inequality, poverty and humiliation that have produced the violence, whether on the world scale or that of our own country.

A world which accepts that the richest 1 per cent will soon own more than half the planet's wealth is heading for a fall, in other words, for that endless violence, without borders or territories, that is the new face of war. And the first to know this, having been subjected to it for so long, are the peoples of the Arab world, whose culture is mainly Muslim. Peoples faced for too long with venal, corrupt states that are indifferent to their needs and offer no prospect of hope to the young, thus giving free rein to terror. How not to question the French responsibility for this impasse, when our own state congratulated itself, in 2014, on a massive increase in the arms sales that now make the obscurantist kingdom of Saudi Arabia France's largest foreign customer?

But the despair is not just far away, and we can no longer pretend to ignore it, turning our eyes away from the spectacle of distress in our streets, on our pavements, or acting as though we never noticed poverty, relegated to what official jargon calls the '*banlieues*', as if they were reservations. We have to be blind to ourselves for it to be so hard to look this reality in the face: just like the two earlier anti-Semitic crimes in Toulouse and Brussels, the three terrorists in the ill-fated month of January 2015 were children of our own society, our nation, our Republic. They were born French; they did not come from somewhere else, but from here.

These murderers are our people. To recall this is by no means to excuse their actions, but quite simply to be a republican. A true republican. Not as a posture but as a demand. Republican like Victor Hugo, pointing out the urgency of the social question in his famous speech on poverty in 1849: 'How can you heal the sickness if you do not inspect the wounds?' 'You have achieved nothing,' he charged the conservative assembly that he sought to shake, 'so long as the spirit of revolution has public suffering as its auxiliary! You have achieved nothing, nothing, so long as in this work of destruction and darkness, which continues underground, the men of evil have unhappy men as their collaborators!' And he concluded, 'Gentlemen, think of this: if anarchy throws open the abyss, it is destitution that dug it.'

Resentment is a bitter motor of History. It is made of unhealed wounds, undigested affronts, brute violence, accumulated humiliations and ancient traumas whose legacy casts a dark shadow. Sufferings that generate the necrosis of hope, a sense of total impasse, of an impossible and inconceivable future. At this point, resentment destroys politics as common welfare and shared existence. Complacent in victimization, those who succumb to it will always seek scapegoats for their despair. Their complaint will come up against walls which they imagine they can only pass by way of destruction, to the point of denying to others the common humanity that has been denied to them. And they do so all the more easily in an interconnected world, shrunken in space and accelerated in time, that offers them the nihilist ideology to fill this existential void on their home computer.

This is a resentment we have constantly fuelled in a section of our people, of our youth. A section that, on a daily basis, no longer experiences a Republic for all. A section that for decades has seen itself stigmatized by its origin, its appearance, its culture, its religion, as if it was distinct, separate, remote and distrusted. A section that was spawned from France's long projection across the world, and has now returned to the European 'America' that is our own country, whose lower classes have always been renewed by waves and mixtures of migrations. A section whose legitimate democratic and social aspirations have been too often disqualified on ethnic or religious pretexts.

This was the meaning of the alarm I sounded with *Pour les musulmans*. Published in September 2014, this book continued *Dire non* [Saying No], an appeal that I published in spring of that year to say no to the 'monsters' of racism and xenophobia, hatred and violence, those morbid phenomena of times of transition and uncertainty, when the old world is dying and the birth of the new one is delayed. 'By showing the people a scarecrow, you create the real monster.' Echoing one warning with another, I have continued since then to cite this phrase from Émile Zola's 1896 pamphlet 'For the Jews' that was my point of departure. In vain, alas, since the publishing and media landscape, through to the attacks of January 2015, was cluttered with Islamophobic pieces, designating our Muslim compatriots, with their diversity of origins, cultures and beliefs, as trouble-makers, devious and menacing invaders whom we should even consider expelling from our – their! – country.

How can we teach our young people respect for others, simple civility, and the unacceptability of insult and offence on the grounds of origin, appearance or belief, when our public space, its media and politicians are busy teaching them the opposite? Instilling an irresponsible transgression that is destructive of any ideal of solidarity, any common Republic or national community? The proclamation of freedom of expression and the defence of the right to caricature, with all its ironic or mocking excesses, that accompanied solidarity with *Charlie Hebdo*, does not mean that our public life should be debased and diverted into hatred for one section of our people by reason of their origin, culture or religion. Hatred cannot hide behind humour.

For the Muslims could just as well have been entitled *For France*. It is an appeal to a common cause, a wake-up call to society so that the Republic can finally be for everyone. An appeal to follow the path of empathy along which, by walking towards the other, you find yourself. An appeal to seek side by side that democratic and social perspective which alone can chase away the looming clouds and storms. To come together and stand up as one around the demand for equality, the equality of rights and opportunities that the current obsession with identity would undo, leaving in its place the ravages of inequality, hierarchy and exclusion.

'France, wake up, think of your glory,' Zola wrote in his 1898 *Lettre à la France*. I borrow from that text the following warning: 'The Republic is invaded by reactionaries of every stripe, they worship it with a brutal and terrible love, they embrace it only to stifle it.' For the author of the famous *J'accuse …!* could conceive the Republic only as something in motion, forever being invented and created anew – the very opposite of the immobilism and conservatism that too often appeal to it as a justification for rejection and fear-mongering. Zola, the son of an Italian immigrant, therefore addressed himself to his country in these words: 'Is this what you want, France, the imperilling of all that you have purchased so dearly, religious tolerance, equal justice for all, the fraternal solidarity of all citizens?'

More than a century later, I put to France that very same question.

Paris, January 2015

Our Enemy Is Fear

On Friday, 13 November 2015, a whole society was the target of terrorism: our society, our France in its diversity and plurality, a France of meetings and mixtures. It was this open society that the acts of terror sought to close; to silence it by fear, to obliterate it beneath the horror. And it is this society that we have to defend, for it is our protection.

A Friday evening in autumn, the weather fine. The weekend, a time for going out, a space of relaxation. A time to enjoy meeting friends, a time for concerts and sports matches. Gatherings of ordinary people, men and women together, youngsters of different nationalities, a variety of pleasures where, according to taste or desire, you can drink, smoke, dance, socialize, mix, seduce, love – in short, go out and meet one another.

These simple words suffice. No grandiloquence is needed to share what we have all felt since yesterday: each one of us, our children, our parents, our friends, our neighbours, we ourselves, were in the murderers' sights.

Because, unlike the January attackers, they did not target obviously symbolic sites to express their hatred of freedom (*Charlie Hebdo*) or hatred of Jews (the HyperCacher super-market); it has been said that the terrorist authors of the Paris butchery did not have a target. But this is a misread-ing. Armed with a totalitarian ideology, in which religious speech serves as an argument to kill all plurality, wipe out all diversity, deny all individuality, their mission was to frighten a society that embodies the opposite promise.

Beyond France, its foreign policy or the policy of its rulers, their target was the democratic ideal of a society of freedom based on rights: the right to have rights, equality of rights without distinction of origin, appearance or belief; the right to make one's way in life regardless of birth or background. A society of individuals, whose 'we' is woven from countless interconnected 'I's'. A society of individual freedoms and collective rights.

To take the proper measure of what is threatened by a terror unprecedented in our country, the most deadly attacks in Europe since those in Madrid in 2004, we have also to measure the challenge that the murderers and their commanders have thrown down to us. The terrorists want to close this open society. Their war aim is that it should clam up, withdraw into itself, divide, shrink, demean itself as it loses its way, in other words, loses itself. It is our collective life that they want to transform into a civil war against ourselves.

Whatever its contexts, epochs or latitudes, terrorism always wagers on fear. Not only the fear that it spreads in society, but the politics of fear it arouses at the summit of the state: a forward flight in which totalitarian terror pushes democracy into a state of emergency, a war without end, without fronts or limits, with no strategic objective other than its own perpetuation, a war of attacks and responses that feed off one another, causes and effects that mingle endlessly with no prospect of a peaceful conclusion.

Painful as it may be, we have to make the effort to grasp the portion of rationality in terrorism – the better to combat it and avoid falling into its trap, rather than acquiesce to its own reasoning out of ignorance or blindness. The wellspring of its terrifying deadly logic is a self-fulfilling prophecy: to use terror to provoke a still greater chaos from which it hopes to reap a further yield of anger, resentment and injustice. Something that we know from recent experience, given that the United States' precipitous reactions to the attacks of 2001 led to the Iraq disaster out of which the so-called Islamic State arose, born from the ruins of a destroyed state and the wounds of a violated society.

Will we be able to learn from these catastrophic errors, or are we going to repeat them? It is clear enough that by that yardstick, in a context of already cumulative crises – economic, social, ecological, European, etc. – our country is living through a historic moment in which democracy is rediscovering tragedy, the fragility of the former imperilled by the passions of the latter. For the immediate stake is not far away, but here in France. We knew, in the wake of the January attacks, that the real test was still to come. This autumn, on retiring from his post, the anti-terrorist judge Marc Trévidic reminded us of this in *Paris-Match*, with a warning that did not spare our rulers: 'Politicians adopt martial postures, but they have no long-term vision ... I do not believe that French strategy is well founded.'

Faced with the peril that concerns us all, we cannot abandon our future and our security to those who govern us. Although it is their task to protect us, we must not let them do so against us, despite us, without us.

It is always difficult to utter disturbing questions, the kind that are still inaudible so soon after the events that gripped a whole people, uniting them in compassion and fright. Collectively, however, we will not be able to durably resist the challenge of terror if we are not in control of the responses brought to it. If we are not informed, consulted, mobilized. If we are denied the right to question a foreign policy of alliances with dictatorial or obscurantist regimes (Egypt, Saudi Arabia) and warlike adventures with no strategic vision (from the Sahel via Libya to Syria); the right to question the accumulation of security laws that prove ineffective (while infringing our liberties); to question short-sighted and ill-considered political speeches (particularly on Islam, made into a scapegoat, with 'assimilation' as the return of the colonial repressed), which divide rather than uniting, which fuel hatred rather than reassuring, which express the fears of those above rather than mobilizing the people below.

To face up to terrorism we have to act as a society, to build up precisely what they want to knock down. To defend our France, our rainbow France with all the power of its diversity and plurality, this France able to make common cause in a rejection of amalgams and scapegoats. This France whose heroes in 2015 have been Muslims as well as atheists, Christians, Jews, freemasons, agnostics, of all origins, cultures and beliefs. The France of Ahmed Merabet, of Algerian origin, the policeman who gave his life outside the *Charlie Hebdo* offices. The France of Lassana Bathily, of Malian origin, the 'illegal' immigrant who saved several hostages at the HyperCacher. The France that showed us, during that long Paris night, so many rescuers, carers, doctors, police, soldiers, fire-fighters, people of goodwill, a thousand solidarities that also sprang from the diversity – human, social, cultural, religious, etc. – that makes up the country's wealth. And its strength.

In Great Britain, at the time of the 2005 attacks, society spontaneously came together around a slogan invented by a young man on the internet: 'We're not afraid.' In Spain, with the attacks of 2004, society spontaneously rallied around the symbol of open palms upraised, unarmed and yet determined.

No, we are not afraid. Except of ourselves, should we give way. Except of our rulers, should they mislead or ignore us. We shall defend, harder than ever, the openness of the society that the killers sought to close. And the symbol of this refusal could be two hands stretched out to clasp each other. Two hands crossed. Two hands connected.

Paris, 14 November 2015